THE ANYANYA MOVEMENT IN SOUTHERN SUDAN

A Frontline Soldier's Perspective

by Francis Barson Yousa

The publisher wishes to acknowledge and thank Dr. Douglas H. Johnson for his invaluable help and support for Africa World Books and its mission of preserving and promoting African cultural and literary traditions and history. Dr. Johnson and fellow historians have been instrumental in ensuring that African people remain connected to their past and their identity. Africa World Books is proud to carry on this mission.

The photo on the front cover shows Lt. Col Simon Jada after his incorporation into the wildlife forces as a major.

Copyright © 2022, Francis Barson Yousa

ISBN: 9780645583281

No part of this publication may be reproduced, stored in a retrieval system, or transmitted, in any form, or by any means, electronic, mechanical, photocopying, recording or otherwise, without the prior permission of the publishers.

This book is sold subject to the conditions that it shall not, by way of trade or otherwise, be lent, re-sold, hired out or otherwise circulated without the publisher's prior consent in any form of binding or cover other than in which it is published and without a similar condition including the condition being imposed on the subsequent purchaser.

Cover design, typesetting and layout: Africa World Books
Unit 3, 57 Frobisher St, Osborne Park, WA 6017
P.O. Box 1106 Osbourne Park, WA 6916

"Out of Anger and Hatred a man chews and eats man's flesh"

TABLE OF CONTENTS

Dedication and Acknowledgement — *ix*
Preface — *xi*
Forward — *xvii*

Chapter 1:
Introduction — 1
History of the Anyanya — 4
The 1955 Torit Mutiny — 14

Chapter 2:
The Beginning of the Anyanya War of Liberation — 23
The Anyanya Officers in Western Equatoria Province — 25
First Encounter with Simon Jada Muludiang — 29
First Discussion with Commander Simon Jada — 34
The 1965 Juba and Wau Massacres — 34

The 112 Seminarians from Kit 38
The Anyanya Camps in Subi Nyambiri,
Group C, and Other Locations 38
Non-Commissioned Officers 40

Chapter 3:
Military Operations 45
Mysterious Incidents in the Camp 57
List of Officers Under Col. Simon Jada's Command 59
Other Activities 64

Chapter 4:
The Behavior and Character of Simon Jada 67
Southern Officers who Perished in the Juba Massacre
of 1992 70

Chapter 5:
The Expulsion of the Missionaries and Forceful
Conversion to Islam 76
The Relationship Between the Anyanya and Idi Amin 77
The Addis Ababa Agreement and the Southern Sudan
Regional Government (1972 – 1983) 80
The Negotiations 86
The Regional Executive Council 92
The Fall of General Jaafar Mohamed el Nimeiri (1985). 98

Conclusion 103

Annex 1: Photos of our gallant heroes who perished in Juba during the war for liberation. 109
Annex 2: Execution orders or decrees from the Arab commander of the Equatoria division 115
Annex 3: Lists of executed martyrs in 1992 118
Annex 4: Abbreviations and Meanings of Words and Phrases 123
Annex 5: List of the south Sudanese intellectuals who were brutally murdered by the Sudanese army 126

Dedication and Acknowledgement

THIS BOOK IS DEDICATED to my lovely family and friends who tirelessly listened to my narrative and corrected or gave me invaluable advice. They helped me with their expertise and advised me on how to go about writing the book. Let me not forget the very delicious food they fed me. I am grateful to my ten children, especially those who are savvy with computers, who helped me in many ways.

I would be remiss if I did not mention my friends, Charles Nathaniel (Abdalla Musa), Dr. James Eluzai, Dr. Awad Mustafa, Col. Dr. Francis Tombe, my friends the generals, advocate Emmanuel Yugusuk, and many others. My friends and colleagues in the office, with whom sometimes we sit under the big neem tree, thank you all. I also want to thank the widows and family members of the martyrs of 1992, for sharing pictures of their loved ones with me. Special gratitude goes to Monsur Akec, director of scholarships in the Ministry of Education of the Republic of South Sudan, and Rufas Joka Samuel.

I am also indebted to all my colleagues in the defunct Jubek State Economic Zone who gave me invaluable advice. I am also grateful to my office manager, Araba George, and his colleagues in the Secretariat of the Insurance Regulatory Authority. I am also indebted to Computer icon, Mr. Stans Tombe and his colleagues who assisted in the organization of the chapters in this booklet. I am of course most grateful, also, to Peter Lual, the publisher of Africa World Books, for releasing this book to the world.

My maternal uncle General (retired) Jackson Jejen Abel also deserves my gratitude and praise. A former captain in the Anyanya based at Nyambiri camp, he gave me invaluable information about the personalities in the Anyanya.

Most importantly, I am greatly indebted and thankful to Lt. General Augustino Jadallah Camillo Wani, who took time out of his busy schedule to read the initial draft of this booklet. I am also grateful to his Deputy, the Advisors, and Ministers, and to all those who advised me in one way or another not to give up this book project.

This book is in memory of my wife late Mama Jersa Kide Barsaba Amin, the Deputy Chairperson of the Country's Election Commission. She was alive at the time of writing, and she contributed greatly both morally and financially. I miss her so much.

Preface

THE OPENING OF A BRIDGE named after Colonel (late) Simon Jada at the Munuki residential area in Juba, in 2019, encouraged me to write a book that discusses the Anyanya and memorializes the life of this tough, diminutive guerrilla commander. Late Jada, who was an Anyanya officer, was murdered in 1992. He was beloved by all his soldiers. He has left behind a strong legacy in this country, and we will remember his heroic deeds forever.

This book tells a portion of the story of the Anyanya as experienced by the author. It is meant to remind us of a time when we collectively fought for our rights as South Sudanese. It also commemorates the Anyanya fighters of the time. The Anyanya legacy in South Sudan is strong. Our president, Salva Kiir Mayardit, was himself an Anyanya fighter. So was our hero Dr. John Garang de Mabior.

The Anyanya was an army of grit and substance. Recruitment

to the Anyanya ranks was a rigorous process. One must be tall, must have muscles, not be excessively plump, must be very quick to decide, very agile, and should have a clean criminal record.

The Anyanya also recruited young men as informers. Their task was to swiftly convey information between the Anyanya camps about the movement of Arab troops advancing to attack the rebel positions. These young men were called scouts. Their job exposed them to the enemy and so many of them often got killed before the actual battle started. Sometimes, they would be betrayed by fellow villagers. But that did not dissuade people from serving in the Anyanya. In my Yangwara community, many young men served as scouts. Young men like Emmanuel Maju, Joseph Gwaki, El Hag Stephen, Hassan Apollo, Nathaniel Wani and Lujang Elisa, are examples of youth who became scouts and later became Anyanya soldiers.

Nevertheless, the killing of South Sudanese by the Arabs was only possible because of Southern collaboration in the effort.[1] South Sudanese should ask themselves the following questions before putting all blame on the Arabs:

1. Did or do northern Sudanese soldiers know who southern Sudanese were/are? The answer is "No".
2. Have they lived long enough in the south to know the southerners very well to be able to identify an Anyanya soldier from a civilian? The answer is a big "No".

---

1   At times, the terms Southern Sudanese and South Sudanese are used interchangeably in this book to mean one and the same thing. Please note after the independence of South Sudan, its people are now called South Sudanese as opposed to Southern Sudanese.

With reference to the betrayals of South Sudanese by South Sudanese, the Arabs use to say we, the South Sudanese kill each other just like "fish eating each other." The Sudanese Arabs never killed any person without proper evidence. Many of them used to say, "You Southerners kill yourselves alone." Indeed, many Arab soldiers, on different occasions used to sympathize with victims and eventually released them.

This book discusses the history of the Anyanya. Many books on the Anyanya have been published, some by academics, and others, by individuals who participated in the struggle. My book falls in the latter category. It is the story of the Anyanya, focusing on key individuals and events as experienced by the author. Within this category, most of the books that have been published, were written by senior Anyanya officers. I joined the Anyanya as a teenage soldier. In that respect, my book is different from that of a high-ranking officer. In this regard, my book augments the literature by describing events through the eyes of a teenage Anyanya soldier.

I joined the Anyanya in 1963, leaving in 1967. I had sneaked into Juba in 1967 but was arrested by the Arabs and spent three days in custody. The Anyanya camp to which I belonged was called Subi camp. Upon my arrest, the camp was on the verge of being relocated for fear that I had compromised its location. Things could have been worse for me during interrogation, but I stuck to one statement until I was released. I think I missed death just by a whisker. After my release, Bari elders advised me to go to school. Also, my elder brother Stephen Soro, who later joined the Anyanya Movement, ordered me to go to school and leave him to continue with the movement.² I was a brilliant student and there was a lot of hope vested in me by the people around me.

It was difficult for me to decide on whether to go to school or return to the movement. I felt that it was shameful to run away from my national duty, the job of real men. But the young Arab Police First Lieutenant who released me from captivity warned me that the security organs were watching my movements closely. If I was ever arrested again and taken to the police as an Anyanya, he would not assist me. I would be executed. He claimed (of course, correctly) that I was indeed an Anyanya soldier but at the same time a student. He was a university graduate and wanted me to graduate too from the University of Khartoum. This kind Arab man and the Bari elders succeeded to convince me, and with a heavy heart, I left for Khartoum by boat in 1967.

Throughout this book, I used the word "Arab" to describe the Sudanese government and its army. I wish to state that the use of this term should not be misconstrued to mean an offence. The army was dominated mainly by Western Sudanese, people from the Nuba Mountains, Ingessana, and South Sudanese. The officers were mainly Northern Sudanese. Arab civilians in the North are generally good people and cooperative. Today, many are regretting their individual actions and the actions of their past governments for atrocities inflicted on the Southerners and the mismanagement of the Southern problem, which culminated in the secession of South Sudan. On a visit to the Sudanese capital prior to the publication

---

2   After the absorption of the Anyanya into the Sudanese army, Stephen was promoted to the rank of Lt. Colonel by the time he died n 1995.

of this book, I met many Arab friends who were very friendly and welcomed me, insisting that I should return to reside in Khartoum. They also regretted the separation of South Sudan and wished for Sudan to be one again. They cited the reunification of Germany after the end of the Cold War as something that could happen to the two Sudans. However, I think that currently, the reunification of the South with the North is of course unthinkable.

Forward

THIS BOOK WAS WRITTEN by Francis Barson Yousa, who was an Anyanya fighter in 1963-1967. Mr. Barson thought it wise to document some facts concerning the seventeen years of civil war in the then Southern Sudan. The war, which was fought all over Southern Sudan, was specifically ferocious in the three Equatoria provinces of the Republic of Sudan. In this book, Francis describes events in one camp called Subi in the center of Central Equatoria province. He was the adjutant to Lt. Colonel Simon Jada Muludiang, the Anyanya commander of the camp, and clerk of the whole camp. Although Francis devotes a good deal of this book on the commander, he also covers a lot of information about the Anyanya movement.

I have known Mr. Barson since 2010/11 when he was appointed Minister of Information, Communication, Youth and Sports, Archives and Antiquities, Tourism and Hotels Management, by the then Governor of Central Equatoria State of the Republic of South Sudan. Francis has been writing pamphlets and reports for the government and the United Nations High Commissioner for Refugees (UNHCR), where he served as Administrative Officer for fifteen years, from 1991 to 2005. He has acquired strong skills in writing and has thus decided to write this booklet on a topic he was well versed in. He has also completed writing a book on his tribe, the Yangwara of South Sudan. These two books are currently undergoing editing and possible printing and publishing.

I personally commend Francis Barson for taking the time to write about the history of our struggle and the Yangwara tribe. These two books will be useful in our schools, colleges, and universities. They document the past and recent histories of our people and events in the nascent Republic of South Sudan, the 193rd state of the world. I thank you all for showing interest in reading this book.

Hon. Stephen Lado Onesimo,
Juba, Republic of South Sudan.

Chapter One

Introduction

IN 1963, THE PEACE which engulfed the whole of South Sudan since the 1955 Torit mutiny was disrupted by gun battles in the bushes of Equatoria Region. The fighting pitted General Ibrahim Aboud's military government against the newly formed troops of the Anyanya guerrilla movement. Earlier in 1962, students of Rumbek and Juba Commercial Senior secondary schools went on political strike. This was followed by intermediate school students in and across Southern Sudan. There was a lot of anti-Arab sentiment, disharmony and hatred, and determination to rid the South of Arab domination. The student revolt resulted in an influx of people into the bushes, a feat for the ranks of the rebel Anyanya. However, many students were asked by the Anyanya to go to neighboring countries to pursue their education.

The reasons why south Sudanese decided to pursue war, are discussed in this book. Notable among them, is the mistreatment Northern Sudanese troops meted on Southerners. Then there is the issue of incompatible religious differences. Northerners are Muslims, while Southerners were largely Christian, with some embracing traditional African beliefs. Muslim Northerners could marry non-Muslim Southern women, who in most cases, would be compelled to convert to Islam. However, Southern men were forbidden from marrying Northern Muslim women. This caused a friction between both communities.

The Anyanya war lasted seventeen years and only came to an end after a series of intensive negotiations were concluded in Addis Ababa in March 1972. In this agreement, Southerners shelved their ambition for an independent state. Instead, they opted for the formation of an autonomous government in the South, which they led. Relative calm engulfed the south after the agreement, despite a few skirmishes by disgruntled Anyanya fighters that took place at Juba airport, Juba barracks, Wau, Nassir and other locations. However, ten years after the Addis Ababa Agreement, a new war broke out again between Sudan Peoples' Liberation Movement/Army, led by John Garang and Jaafar Nimeiri's government in Khartoum. This war was brutal and more destructive than the first war. It lasted for twenty-one years and only came to an end after serious negotiations in Naivasha, Kenya.

Anthropologists describe the South Sudanese as the tall, ebony skinned, black people inhabiting the vast stretch of land south of Kosti town in the White Nile State of Sudan. Their land stretches southwards up to the borders with Uganda and Congo. In the east, their country is bordered by Ethiopia and Kenya. In the west, with Congo and the Central African Republic; and of course, western Sudan north of the South Sudanese town of Aweil. The major tribes in this vast, but sparsely populated land, are the Dinka, Nuer, Shilluk, Azande, Bari, Yangwara, Latuka, Lango, Peri (Lokoro), Toposa, Murle, Didinga, Ngepo, Tenet, Pojulu, Kakwa, Moru, Baka, Avukaya, Mundu, Makaraka, Lugbara, Keliko, Madi, Acholi, Balanda, Bongo, Ndogo, Kreish, Kuku, Boya, Jur Chol, Jur Bel, Kachipo, Brun, Tenet, to mention but a few. These tribes are scattered all over the large South Sudanese territory and are mainly agriculturists and pastoralists. Those in towns are government officials/workers or traders.

In contrast, the Northern Sudanese Arabs are light skinned, and are a mixture of the African negroid race, which dominated the Sudan in the early centuries, and Arabs who immigrated from the Arabian Peninsula. The Arab immigrants found African kingdoms in the Sudan. An example is the Kush Kingdom, which is also mentioned in the Bible. The Arab invasion of Sudan resulted in the birth of this unique race (half negroid and half Arab). The people in Mourada locality of Omdurman can confirm this fact. The slave trade of the past centuries, saw Africans from South Sudan ferried into Northern Sudan and beyond by slave traders who were mostly Arabs encouraged by Europeans. The inhabitants of Buri, Jereif, and Mourada neighborhoods in Khartoum are descendants of slaves. Legend has it that Jereif is said to be the name of a Shilluk chief who was resident in what is now called Jerief east and Jerief west.

The word Khartoum is said to be a distortion of a Dinka word "Khiertom," meaning the trunk of an elephant, that is to say, the confluence of the two Niles, the Blue and the White Niles.

History of the Anyanya

The Anyanya movement was an off shoot of the Torit mutiny of August 1955 in Southern Sudan. This mutiny built on grievances that date back to the 1947 Juba Conference[3] when Southern leaders, who had little formal education, refused to accept the Sudanization program on the basis that the South was still ill-prepared to be paired in a joint government with the North.

Nevertheless, the contentious relationship between Southerners and Northerners dates to the advent of the Turko-Egyptian era in Sudan in 1821. An assortment of Turks, Egyptians, Europeans, and Northerners penetrated the South for slave-raiding purposes. The defeat of the Turko-Egyptian administration by the Mahdiya in 1885 did not stop the slave trade in Southern Sudan. Mahdist forces continued excursions into Southern Sudan in search of slaves, ivory, ostrich feathers, and natural resources.

---

3   The building where the conference took place is still present in Hai Neem near Khor Bou stream. As the Minister of Culture and Archives in the Central Equatoria government of HE Governor Clement Wani Konga in 2012, I attempted to change the house from an official residence to an archives unit which would indeed be an historical site that tourists would be encouraged to visit. The attempt failed due to the intransigence of the official occupying the building who flatly refused to move out.

The defeat of the Mahdist regime in 1898 opened the path for the establishment of Condominium rule by Britain and Egypt over the Sudan. It was during this era that a sense of Sudanese nationalism was born. Early propagators of this nationalism include Ali Abdel Latif (of Dinka origin) and his compatriot Abdel Fadil El Maz, and others, who organized an uprising against British rule in 1924. Ali Abdel Latif formed what was called the White Flag League which was dedicated to drive the British from Sudan. The activities of the League were suppressed, and its leaders were arrested and sent to prison.

By the late 1940s, European colonialism was generally becoming untenable. The colonial masters in some jurisdictions in Africa, began thinking of handing over power to African leaders. In Sudan, the 1947 Juba Conference constituted such an effort that was designed to prepare locals for independence. This process picked up steam with the launch of the "Sudanization" process in 1954.

In the Juba Conference of 1947, it was clear that the equation was unbalanced as the North was represented by highly educated individuals, while Southern Sudan was represented by less sophisticated leaders with only a few years of formal education. Mohd Saleh El Shingite, a trained lawyer, led the Northern side against the uneducated but intelligent chiefs and few educated Southerners (Chief Lolik Ladu, Hon. Clement Mboro, Daniel Jumi and others).

The Sudanization process culminated in Sudan's independence in 1956. But before Sudan's independence, southern politicians unanimously supported the formation of a federal system of government. The Northern political elites deceitfully agreed to the demand. However, after attaining Sudan's independence, they dishonored the agreement and forced the South to accept a unitary system of government. Nowhere is this sense of betrayal captured more aptly than in the book "Too many agreements dishonored," written by the soft-spoken Abel Alier.

Northern elites' rejection of a federal system of government was followed by a clampdown on Southern leaders. In 1960 and 1962, following rumors of their impending arrest, the Southern politicians fled into exile in neighboring countries. This was followed by the exodus of thousands of Southerners into exile. In exile, the exiled politicians formed a political front to confront the Sudanese regime. The Sudan African National Union (SANU) led by Hon. Joseph Oduho, was formed in Uganda in 1963. To appease the Southerners, the military ruler General Ibrahim Aboud appointed an elderly Southerner, Hon. Santino Deng Teng, as a minister of animal resources. He held the post for ten years. Many Northerners referred to Southerners derogatively as animals. As such, Southerners viewed the animal resources portfolio as an insult to them.

At the same time, the Arabs were fond of addressing southerners and Nubas of Kordofan as "Abid" meaning slaves. This infamous Arabic word was widely used by the northern Sudanese but was vehemently detested by the southerners/Nubas sometimes to the point of physical confrontations. Indeed many Southerners and Nubas were used as slaves in Arab families. The Nubas were specifically employed as garbage cleaners including carrying buckets full of human waste to be dumped somewhere outside the city of Khartoum.

President Jaafar Mohamed Nimeiri tried his best to abolish the use of this word (Abid) with little success; and as it persisted, there was no other option except to wage the wars for liberation as southerners were reminded continuously of the infamous slave trade of the past centuries. After 1963, Southerners took up arms and started military operations against Sudanese government troops.

The Southern leaders of the time were:

1. Clement Mboro, a Fertit from Bahr el Ghazal (who later became Interior Minister in the government of Sir El Khatim El Khalifa) in Khartoum.
2. Politician Paul Lugali, an elderly, tough Bari statesman who was one of those vying for a federal system of government in the Sudan.
3. Marko Rume (Kuku by ethnicity), the man who initiated student strikes in Southern Sudan in the 1960s.
4. Daniel Jumi, the Bari politician who sent a telegram to all Southern soldiers in South Sudan to prepare for difficult times ahead (meaning an uprising). He and others were jailed but later escaped to neighboring Congo.
5. Politician Benjamin Lwoki, a politician from the Pojulu, who became a Minister in the Azhari government after independence.
6. Stanislaus Paysama, from Bahr el Ghazal, who was in the first post-independence government of Sudan.
7. Ahmed Morgan, a Muslim Dinka politician who was in the Liberal party of Southern Sudan.
8. Buth Dieu, a Nuer politician who became a member of the post-independence cabinet.

Clement Mboro   *Benjamin Lwoki*   *Benjamin Lwoki*

Buth Dieu   *Abdel Rahman Sule*   *Father Satrunino Lohure*

Gordon Mourta   *Eliaba James Surur*   *Hillary Paul 'Dogale*

9. Sayed Abdel Rahman Sule, a Bari Muslim who was Chairman of the Liberal Party of Southern Sudan, and others who became members of Parliament in Khartoum.

Also of greater significance was the younger generation of Southern leaders comprising of the following:

10. Father Saturnino Lohure, (Latuko) a Catholic priest who became a politician and a fighter but was betrayed by the Ugandan government and later killed near the Uganda-Sudan border.
11. Gordon Mourtat, a Dinka politician who refused to recognize the Addis Ababa Agreement.
12. Eliaba James Surur, (Pojulu), a career politician who fought in the Anyanya movement and became Chairman of the People's Progressive Party during the Regional Government in Southern Sudan and Deputy Speaker in the Sudanese Parliament of 1988/89.
13. There was also the shrewd and highly respected Bari politician Hillary Paul Lugali, (son to Hon. Paul Lugali mentioned above), chairman of the Southern Front, the only major political party in the country for Southern Sudanese after the demise of the Aboud regime in 1965. He was also a cabinet minister in the Khartoum civilian government of Prime Minister El Sadiq Abdel Rahman El Mahdi (1968/69) and that of Nimeiri in 1969–1983 (Addis Ababa agreement inclusive).
14. Another politician and soldier was Akot Atem (Dinka), deputy defence minister in the rebel administration of Chairman Aggrey Jaden (1963-64).[4]

4　　He visited the Anyanya Headquarters on the Uganda/Sudan border.

15. Enock Mading De Garang, a Dinka politician, was the spokesperson for the rebel Anyanya government in Europe. He was based in Britain and after the Addis Ababa Agreement, became the minister of information in the then regional government of Abel Alier (1972).
16. There was also Dr. Lawrence Wol Wol, a smart (Dinka), graduate of a French university, who became minister of finance and commerce later in the government of Abel Alier too.
17. Another politician who became a cabinet Minister in the government of Abel Alier was Lawrence Lual Lual.
18. Politician Oliver Albino Batali was appointed a cabinet Minister in the government of Abel Alier and later in Nimeiri's Khartoum government when Lagu assumed the presidency of Southern Sudan after the re-division of the south.
19. Isaiah Kulang was another politician who served in the government of Abel Alier as Minister of Communications and Roads.
20. Politician Ezekiel Kodi was appointed Minister in Abel Aier's government.

He went to Nyambiri camp in Equatoria, organized and personally supervised the trial of a Dinka officer who mutinied against the leadership of the movement. After the military tribunal, the verdict, which was death by firing squad, was sent to Mr. Arkangello Barry Wanji, the defense minister, who was stationed in the command headquarters for approval. The response was not in favor of the death sentence; but it arrived too late. The victim was executed despite pleas for clemency. Commander Akot exuded a strong anti-Arab sentiment, but he was fair to all in Southern Sudan, regardless of ethnicity.

Enock Mading De Garang

Lawrence Wol Wol

Premier Ismail El Azhari

Premier Abdalla Bey Khalil

Prime Minister Sir El Khatim El Khalifa

Ezekiel Kodi

Oliver Albino

Isaiah Kulang

Gen. Jaafar Mohd Nimeiri

Ambassador Francis Mading Deng

Molana Hassan Abdalla Turabi

Abel Alier

Gen. Dr. John Garang de Mabior

Gen. Salva Kiir Mayardid

21. Politician Severino Fuli (Madi, brother to Joseph Lagu) was very instrumental in the regional assembly in deciding the fate of the South.

Ismail El Azhari was the first Prime Minister of Sudan. Abdalla Bey Khalil followed briefly as prime minister until he was ousted by General Ibrahim Aboud in 1958. Aboud was then removed from power in October 1964 after a bloody civilian uprising resulting in the appointment of the educationist Sir El Khatim El Khalifa as prime minister in 1964-65. A round table conference was held in Juba in 1965 and extended to Khartoum to discuss the Southern problem; but it failed. It was by then that the Southerners decided to go for war as the only option to gain their freedom.

The lull in fighting (1964-65) between Southern insurgent forces under the Anyanya was broken when Premier Mohamed Ahmed Mahgoub took over the reins of power in 1966-67. Military jet fighters and bombers were sent to spray the Southern towns and forests with bullets and bombs. Casualties were many. This scenario continued during the government of Prime Minister El Sadiq El Mahdi (1967/69) with Bor town suffering the most when Defense Minister Ahmed El Mahdi ordered the annihilation of the chiefs in the town.

The 1955 Torit Mutiny

On 18th August 1955, the Equatoria Corps of the Sudan Defense force (in other words, soldiers from number two company) received orders transferring them to Northern Sudan. All officers and Non-Commissioned Officers (NCOs) were to be relocated to Northern Sudan. My father, a corporal in the Mechanical Transport Department, was a driver among them. My relatives and I were in Torit by then (five boys and a few elderly persons) when the first bullet signaling the mutiny was shot. The mutiny spread quickly like wildfire to all the major towns of Equatoria where Northern officials and soldiers were lynched. The British refused to intervene, and order was only restored on August 31st when the government in Khartoum sent Northern troops to suppress the mutiny.

My father, Corporal Yousa Lado, was in Juba when the rebellion started. He had to drive to Torit to search for his family. By then I and many others had fled from Torit to Magwi. Crossing the

River Kinetti, which had then flooded, was a big risk and I almost drowned. I was only seven years old then and was only saved from drowning because I clung tightly to someone's leg. This person also tried to prevent me from clinging on his leg in the middle of the river. At the bank of the river, the man realized that I was related to him, and he was deeply shocked. He helped me get out of the water. Many people, who could not swim, also drowned.

The reasons for the mutiny were many but a few are mentioned below:
1. Before the transfer of the Equatoria Corps to Khartoum, the British officers in the army were replaced by Northern Sudanese officers causing uneasiness among the Southern soldiers.
2. Rumors were circulated that on arrival in Khartoum, the troops would all be annihilated.
3. Politicians Buth Diu and Sirisio Iro got wind of the fact that Battalion No. 2 was to be moved northwards, to be dispersed into various units in Northern Sudan. They informed Sergeant Saturnino of No. 2 Company about the ill intentions of the Arabs.
4. Soldiers of No. 2 Company were instructed to refuse the transfer and disobey orders. Thus, marking the beginning of the rebellion.
5. The attitude and behavior of the Northern officers was detested by the Southern soldiers. It was said that the Prime Minister sent an order via telegraph that authorized the suppression of Southerners in the South.
6. The Sudanization of the civil service mainly benefited Northern elites, excluding the few educated southerners who were to occupy junior positions.

7. Lastly, but not least, the famous massacre of demonstrators in the Nzara Multi-Purpose Agro factory in Azande land.

There were a few Southern officers in Number Two Company. The most senior was 2nd Lt. Emidio Tafeng Odongi. He had been scheduled for a transfer to Khartoum. Lt. Tafeng was in Juba when the first bullet was shot. According to him and many others, if he were in Torit, the town would have been captured by the Southern troops. Another officer, Lt. David Dada Logunu (Vittorio Logunu) was on holiday in Bilinyang when war broke out. He later fled to join others in Congo to form the Anyanya Movement. There was Lt. Paul Ali Gbattala of Number One Company, who later joined the Anyanya army in Western Equatoria. An officer called Albino was the commander who gave orders for the execution of all the Arab officers. His demise is not known, but some people say he was later executed when the Arab soldiers arrived. Lt. Samuel Abu John, who was commissioned as an officer in 1953, was in Khartoum.

The mutiny suffered from organizational challenges, and it was, quickly suppressed. It was not properly coordinated. The few officers in the corps were scattered and the Southern political leaders were in Khartoum busy with politics, lobbying fervently for a federal system, which was totally rejected by the Arabs; and most importantly, the disorder affected mostly Equatoria province. Bahr el Ghazal province was slightly affected but Upper Nile province was hardly affected. The mutineers retired to their villages, and some crossed into the neighboring countries.

Joseph Oduho   *Aggrey Jaden*   *William Deng Nhial*

On the political side, there were strong leaders like:
- Joseph Oduho. He became a minister in the regional government of Abel Alier in 1973.
- Ezbon Mundiri Gwanja. He later chaired the Anyanya negotiation team during the Addis Ababa talks and became the minister of communication and transport in the same government. Prior that, he was minister of transport and communication in the civilian government of Prime Minister Sir El Khatim El Khalifa in Khartoum in 1964/65. A Moru by tribe, Mundiri was a tall man and determined man in the fight against the injustices of the Arabs, to the extent he would use his fists to fight them although he was a minister. He went as far as stopping Southern women who the Arabs claimed were their wives from going to the North. This usually happened when the Arabs were being transferred to the North. Ezbon would station himself in the river port in Juba and directed the police to stop any Arab from taking any woman to the

North. After joining the Anyanya when he was removed from the government in Khartoum, Ezbon Mundiri led a platoon of Moru guerrilla youths to chase the Arabs from Jambo village in Amadi using mostly bows and arrows and home-made guns made by an Anyanya commander called Hitler. Many Moru youths died but they managed to chase the enemy soldiers from Jambo station.

- Aggrey Jaden, an executive officer-turned politician was another leader who chaired the Sudan African National Union (SANU) in exile. He is said to be the first Southerner to enter and graduate from the University of Khartoum.
- William Deng Nhial was a district commissioner, turned politician who led the Sudan African National Union (SANU) in Khartoum. Previously he was in Kampala (Uganda). He was assassinated in Tonj (South Sudan) in 1968 by forces of the government in Khartoum.

In 1964 when the Aboud regime was toppled, the Southerners in Khartoum rioted when the scheduled arrival of Clement Mboro, a Southerner and minister of interior, at the airport in Khartoum was delayed. They broke property and fought vigorously with the police. Many people were killed and thus all the southerners were assembled in Khartoum football stadium awaiting transportation back to the South. Ezbon Mundiri Gwanja played a big role in transporting these Southerners home.

It was after one or two weeks that my father finally managed to locate us after the mutiny in Torit. He found us in Magwi. We then started the long journey to our village Rokon in western Juba. All the soldiers dispersed to their villages after the mutiny and after killing several Arab officers and merchants in Torit. The mutineers spared Arabs married to Southerners. One officer by the name of Mohammed El Hag was spared as his mother was a Southern woman and he was requested to hide. Unfortunately, El Hag decided to shoot at a Moru soldier, intending to kill but only wounded him. When this was discovered, he was arrested and executed. The Latuho officer who carried out the executions was Lt. Albino, whose fate is unknown. He either left the country or he was executed by the Arabs later.

The first bullet in Torit was shot by an Arab officer by the name of Salah who wounded his driver (a southern soldier) and fled to Juba. Some people say the fighting started in Juba airport sparking the mutiny in the whole of the south. To be exact, the fighting started in Nzara (Western Equatoria) when workers of the Nzara Complex went on strike in 1955 protesting working conditions and salaries. Several people were either killed or wounded by riot police. Word reached Torit, Juba and Wau that the Arabs had started annihilating southerners. Reports say a soldier from Torit who arrived Yei together with the southern policemen in the town arrested the District Commissioner and killed him burning his body. The deceased DC was at fault because, on hearing about the trouble in Torit, he paraded the policemen with the aim of disarming them and perhaps eliminating them. Similarly, in other smaller towns in Equatoria, Southern policemen and soldiers rampaged through the bushes of the south looking for Arabs. It was pathetic, but the rebels justified their actions by saying the Arabs started the war and should leave the south.

Rumbek Secondary School was closed due to the mutiny which had affected all the towns in South Sudan except a few. The students from Equatoria, specifically Juba had to be transported to their homes. Their Headmaster, an Arab and his family was with them in the truck. The students protected them all the way from Rumbek and never allowed any rebel to approach them. However, at Lainya, a man approached the truck and asked if there were any Arabs on board. He saw the headmaster and ordered him to disembark. A student tried to protect the headmaster, but immediately without warning, got one of his ears cut off with a sharp knife. The students dispersed in fear, and the headmaster was lynched. His wife and kids were spared. When the Arab soldiers eventually arrived from Juba, they arrested many civilians and killed the man who killed the headmaster. They took the deceased's wife to Juba.

I am narrating this incident to indicate the volume of anger and hatred that the Southerners harbored toward the Arabs to the point of harming one of their sons. Note that the student harmed was from the same tribe of the killer.

After fifteen days walk through the forests of Eastern Equatoria via Lobonok in western Bari, my family reached their village, Rokon. Up to Lobonok, they were in the company of Sergeant Gordon Bosok, a Bari who had one rifle which he should have handed over to my father, but he declined. My father had to get another gun. The family continued with their trip on foot to

Rokon through Kagwada, crossing River Nile from Duli, and then to Wonduruba, Miri, and finally to Rokon.

The new British Governor-General, Sir Alexander Knox Helm, declared a state of emergency and ordered the mutineers to lay down their arms. The Arabs used the British to convince the Southern revolutionaries to obey the order to surrender. A small Cessna plane flew over the whole of Equatoria announcing in the various Equatorian languages that the war was over, and all soldiers had to report to their barracks. Anybody who harbored a rebel soldier was to be arrested and executed. That made the relative in whose house we were staying to say we should leave his residence altogether. We ended up in a ramshackle house, which belonged to my father's uncle and my grandmother, who were old and sick. Then my father decided to return to Juba.

Order was not restored immediately until the Northern troops arrived. The Northern soldiers started to execute the mutineers systematically, forcing scores of them to retreat to mountain terrains and organize armed resistance. The mutiny also resulted in the transfer of Juba Commercial and Rumbek senior secondary schools (the only secondary schools in the South) to the North. The mutiny precipitated the beginning of several-decades of guerrilla warfare in the Sudan, culminating in South Sudan's independence in 2011.

At Rokon, there was an Arab merchant by the name of Abbas. The residents of Rokon wanted him dead but no one had the guts to kill him. The residents wanted to use bows and arrows to do the job. Instead, they looted his shop and later, when the Arab army came to Rokon, all those who looted were sent to prison in Juba after surrendering the goods they stole. However, a Yangwara policeman in Maridi traveled all the way to Rokon and shot the merchant with a gun.

My father, in the company of Wilson Laku Musa, the man who killed the Arab merchant at Rokon, arrived Gorom near Luri in Juba. My father then cautioned Laku to flee to Uganda since he had killed an Arab. The Arab government in Juba would not spare his life. Laku refused, reasoning that since his elder brother was already in custody because of him, he was not going to run away and let his elder brother Andrea Nyiki to be killed. Then one night he was captured and taken into custody in Juba. A military tribunal was formed to try Laku. He was sentenced to death by firing squad. The courageous gentleman was then executed together with a Mundari soldier called Nyombe Malo and others near Jebel Kujur (Korok), a hill west of Juba. My father, and many others including officer Tafeng were sent to prison with hard labour in Suakin near Port Sudan, where they extracted salt for almost nine years. My father was freed in 1963 when I was already a student in Mundri Intermediate School.

Chapter Two

The Beginning of the Anyanya War of Liberation

EIGHT YEARS AFTER the Torit mutiny was crushed, remnants of the mutineers were joined by ordinary citizens and many students who revolted and went on strike, to form a new rebellion called the Anyanya movement. The aim of this rebel movement was to continue the fight for freedom from Northern Sudan. As soon as the fighting started in Central Equatoria, specifically in Kajokeji and Tore, General Ibrahim Aboud, who had seized power from the post-independence civilian government, dispatched army generals to the three provinces of Southern Sudan with directives to crush the rebellion. Equatoria Province was specifically under the command of Major General El Tahir Abdel Rahman El Magboul. By then, the Anyanya movement had started ambushing vehicles travelling on the roads to the rural districts. Eventually, the general became friendly to many South Sudanese and targeted only real guerrillas. He was replaced by Major General Ahmed El Tigani, who adopted a hardline stance and was persistent in his will to crush the Anyanya. He failed in his task and shortly after the entire military junta of Ibrahim Aboud was overthrown in a popular civilian uprising led by university students, trade unions, women, youth and other popular organizations. Many people died as a result; prominent among the victims was student Taha el Gorashi, who became a symbol of revolution and democracy. The University of Khartoum was thus considered a springboard for revolutionary movements and activities.

The series of revenge killings and political upheavals in the South that were mentioned earlier, culminated in deep hatred against the North. In 1963, the Anyanya started sporadic shooting all over Equatoria region, beginning with the attack on Kajokeji garrison and the attempt to destroy the Tore Bridge on the Yei-Maridi road. Both attacks met with stiff resistance from the government forces and the bridge was not broken due to the inexperience of the rebels as fighters.

Marko Rume was one of the architects of the student strikes of 1962/63, urging students to go to the bush to form a guerrilla movement against the government. He promised the students that weapons were coming from Israel. Students from Rumbek Secondary school went on strike in 1962/63. This was followed by the strike of the intermediate schools in the South. Students went back to their villages, returning after several months to school.

Others never returned but crossed the borders to Uganda, Congo, and Central African Republic. The bulk of them just remained in the bushes and helped establish military camps for the Anyanya movement. In 1963, Students in Mundri Intermediate School went on strike, protesting the quality of food served in the school. In truth it was a political strike. As one of the best students in my class, I was promoted to the final year. I was one of the ring leaders in the strike, and for that I was dismissed from school. I left for my village and then proceeded to Juba where I campaigned to be readmitted to my school. I wrote a letter to Mr. Hamed Ali Shash, the Governor of Equatoria province. The Governor referred the letter to Mr. Mohamed Ahmed Medani, the education officer of the province for positive action. Before the result could come out, I travelled to the village of Sure, just 50 miles from Juba on the Yei road.

The Anyanya Officers in Western Equatoria Province

1. Lt. Samuel Abu John Kabasi had graduated from the Military College in Wadi Saydna and remained in the North. He was one of the officers in the Southern Corps in 1955. He later joined the Anyanya movement in Western Equatoria.
2. Lt. Paul Ali Gbattala was another officer in Torit in 1955 and later formed the Anyanya brigade in Western Equatoria. He declined to return to town after the Addis Ababa Agreement until he died. Lt. Gbattala was well known for using rituals in his ambushes against Arab convoys. For example he would put an

empty tin in the middle of the road which could not be lifted at all. When the Arabs would stop to investigate and throw the tin away, Lt. Ali would open fire on them inflicting casualties.

3. Officer Dominic Kasiano Bakheit, who was promoted to colonel after the integration of the Anyanya forces and later became a member of the Revolutionary Command Council in 1989, following the coup led by Omar El Bashir.
4. Officer Philip Ayoub, integrated as a Lt. Colonel.
5. Officer Alison Manani Magaya, who was promoted later to colonel and eventually to general. He became the Military Commander of Equatoria Division and eventually governor of Equatoria Region.
6. Officer Dominic Dabi integrated and progressed to colonel in the Sudanese Army.
7. The feared young officer Isaiah Paul who was integrated as a colonel and became Commander of the Presidential Guard during Nimeiri's government. He was one of the few officers who saved President Nimeiri from the reactionary forces of the attempted coup of 1973 led by Colonel Hassan Hissein and the so-called mercenaries (patronized by El Sadiq El Mahdi) of 1976 from Libya led by Brigadier General Mohamed Nour Saad. The two attempted coups were thwarted by Isaiah's strong presidential guards and Major Abul Gassim Mohamed Ibrahim's soldiers who marched to the palace and the radio station in Omdurman. Colonel Isaiah progressed and became a major general. He passed on in the late 1990s.

8. Officer Habakuk Soro was integrated as a junior officer but progressed to the rank of a colonel. He later became the Minister of Wildlife in the Regional government of 1972.
9. Officer Stanley Mazinda was integrated into the army and progressed to the rank of brigadier general.
10. Officer Joseph Vito was also integrated and rose to the rank of colonel in the army.
11. Officer John Mambia promoted to colonel in the army.
12. The Anyanya Lieutenant John Masua Madanza was integrated into the army and eventually ended up as a general in the Sudanese armed forces. He became the security advisor to Governor Alison Manani Magaya.

The Officers in the Amadi District (Moru camps) of The Anyanya Movement (Western Equatoria) were as follows:
13. Officer Engineer Scopas Juma (later promoted to major general in the Engineering Corps of the Sudanese Army).
14. Officer Arnold Mamur Dangura (promoted to rank of colonel in the Sudanese Army).
15. Officer Christopher Dobili (promoted to Lt. Colonel in the Army). He escaped death from the White House in Juba (the human butchery in the military barracks) where he was jailed, but he managed to jump over the fence through the help of a Good Samaritan, who was a soldier.
16. Prominent was the famous Major Sunday Borge (promoted later to brigadier general) who released the ill-fated Fokker Plane that crashed in the bushes of Mundri in the Moru land,

but fortunately most of the passengers escaped death. In the plane were several Arab soldiers, policemen and merchants. Prominent among them were General (Police) Hassab al Rusul and merchant Al Tayeb of Juba market. Col. Dobili came face to face with the Arab police chief who was so frightened that he earlier took out the police uniforms and hid them. The colonel recognized him, saluted the police chief and told him to put on his uniform and all the Anyanya soldiers were ordered to respect the Arab officer. He didn't believe that he was going to be released with all the others. They were then taken to Owingybul to meet General Joseph Lagu, leader of the Anyanya. The passengers were later freed and taken to Juba. They were all about thirty in number including Southerners and Arab soldiers and merchants from Khartoum. The prominent Southerner in the group was Sayed Sadiq Fargalla (a Muslim who was mistaken to be another CID Bari Muslim chief of the same name but was spared and freed also).

17. Lieutenant Elikana Tiger progressed to the rank of colonel and later joined the SPLA from Damazine.
18. Officer Boniface Bwona Andragu became a colonel in the army and was mostly working in Northern Sudan.
19. Officer Levrick Lewa was also integrated into a senior rank in the army.
20. Officer Ezekiel Watts was integrated into the prisons forces as a senior officer.
21. Officer Christopher Juma (Avukaya) was integrated into the army as a senior officer. He later became a priest in the

Episcopal Church of South Sudan.
22. Officer Jecke Garanya was believed to be using magic to fight the Arabs.
23. Officer Edward Luda became a lieutenant in the army.

Many Yangwara and Mundari youths and students joined the Moru camps. One of them was student Emmanuel Ija Baya, a Mundari, who is now a medical doctor.

Elsewhere in Eastern Equatoria, there were legendary individuals, (both military and civilians) like officers Lutada, Lohiyoro, Lolika and others who fled to the top of Imatong Mountain and gave the Arabs a hard time shooting at them from the mountain. Many other officers and men remained outside South Sudan and formed the Anyanya movement.

First Encounter with Lt. Col. Simon Jada Muludiang

It was on Sunday in 1964 when I entered the village of Sure. My uncle the late Ustaz Martin Rego was a village schoolteacher in Sure School. They were praying in the church when I arrived. I decided to proceed to my uncle's house a few hundred meters away. At a corner, I met a man in ragtag uniform approaching from the front. As he was about to pass, the man stopped me and asked in a rude manner where I was coming from and where I was going to. I replied sternly that it was none of his business. He looked straight into my eyes indicating authority. Suddenly from the rear, more than ten people emerged carrying shot guns, rifles,

Lt. Col. Simon Jada Muludyang

and pistols. It now dawned on me that I had come face-to-face with the Anyanya. Seeing that I was frightened, these men took me back to the school, and made me sit under a tree for interrogation. One of them a short man dressed in a well pressed khaki uniform with a pistol strapped to his waist, barked an order for me to be thoroughly searched and interrogated. I immediately knew that the man in khaki was the leader in command. My interrogator was a slightly tall, middle-aged man in police uniform who knew a bit of the English language. He ran through my bag throwing out all the contents and reading the papers and letters inside. My heart jumped into my mouth when I realized that I had brought along a copy of the letter which I wrote to Governor Ali Shash requesting to go back to school, otherwise I would join those bad men who were fighting in the bush (the Anyanya). If the letter was discovered, I thought I was going to be dead meat. But the interrogator skimmed through and announced that those were all school materials. Perhaps he did not read it well or he just wanted to save me. The man was previously a police security man in the Sudanese police before joining the Anyanya. His name was Quirino Dini. Later, he fell out of favor and the commander tortured him, calling him a CID (meaning government informer).

After a while, I proceeded to my uncle's house and went to bed. My uncle came and after getting the news of the arrest, insisted that I should join the movement. After a while one of the Anyanya soldiers asked me to see them. I complied and they offered me a drink, locally brewed beer (merisa), which I declined. They then asked me to join them. After some persuasion, I agreed to join them, even though I was too young to be in an army. The group left for Kagwada, and I left for Juba to collect my uncle's salary. After two weeks, I returned to Sure and waited for the Anyanya to come.

A serious incident that sparked the execution of women and men alleged to be poisoning others, took place in Kagwada. One tough, tall, and experienced young Anyanya soldier called Sindiu died because he was poisoned. An order was then issued that men and women who poison people, locally known in the Bari language as "kasumak," were to be executed without trial.

Two days later, in the company of the Anyanya soldiers, I left for Subi Camp. Subi is situated in the middle of the mountain which stretches from the Yei-Juba road through the forests of southern Bari. One must travel more than 20 miles southwards, climbing hills and dropping on the other side of the mountain to find River Subi. The Camp is at the bank of this stream which runs southwards from the high lands in Lainya. It is surrounded by the highlands north of Yei town from its southern end. In the southeast one finds the Limbe-Kajokeji road, and in the north are the Bari highlands of Lobonok and Karpeto. Subi Camp is in a very strategic location where the superior armed Arab soldiers could not penetrate. However, in later years, the army managed to destroy Subi camp after fighting for many days which ended in the defeat of the rebels as they ran out of bullets.

The houses in the camp were built from dry wood and grass. The grass-thatched tukuls were covered with leaves for camouflage against military planes. No fire was allowed in the camp except cooking fire under huge trees. No torches were allowed.

Life in the camp in the early days of establishment was very precarious. Although food was scarce, there was plenty of clean running water in the stream. Diseases, ranging from malaria to stomach ailments, were rampant. Because there was no medicine to treat the ill, and lack of food, death lurked around the corner. Shooting accidents were also prevalent. I almost died because of friendly fire; a bullet missed my neck by an inch.

Food was supplied by the citizens in the villages. Troops were sent to the surrounding homesteads (miles away) to meet the chiefs and elders to supply the camp with food items. Those had to be carried by people from each village. Under no circumstances should a soldier rob food from the citizens. Such action would result in a trial by a military tribunal, which would lead to severe punishment.

It was only when the soldiers managed to acquire cattle (collected from Juba vicinity) that the villagers were somehow spared a little bit from food collection. Some of the soldiers also embarked on cultivation, though on small scale subsistence farming on individual basis. Soldiers also ate wild fruits, wild roots, grasshoppers, and alligators (warral in Arabic), pythons, a delicious type of flies (called ngongo in Juba Arabic), and cobras.

Peng Kimang, which means quench the fire in Bari, was a new camp opened in Kajokeji near the Sudan /Uganda border and commanded by Officer Yosea Lokeji, (who was replaced by Col. Bismark Bunit after his death), assisted by Capt. Eyobo Buli and Enoka Kenyi. It was reinforced by soldiers from Subi, Group C and Nyambiri. I want to discuss a bit about some of the individuals in the camp. Sgt. Murrahtore Tombe Kenyi, a Bari from Bilinyang, was a very tall well-built soldier with long strong jaws and very strong muscles. He could handle the Bren gun just like a pop gun. He was sent on mission to Peng Kimang in Kajokeji. There, he misbehaved by messing himself up with women. The following day he wanted to join some fighters who were about to go for patrol duty but was restrained. He insisted and was eventually killed in an ambush on Kajokeji road in confrontation with an Arab patrol. As he was about to die, he shouted to his colleagues to pick the gun which they did as it was considered more important than life. The Arabs celebrated when they saw a tall Anyanya officer lying dead. They assumed that was commander Simuni.

First Discussion with Commander Simon Jada

One day, as I was seated under a huge mahogany tree cleaning my rifle, Commander Simon Jada approached the group. The nearest sergeant barked an order for attention and saluted. The commander saluted back and barked the stand-at-ease order. Simuni beckoned me to follow him into a makeshift grass-thatched building and asked me to sit on a wooden bench. He showed me some books, exercise books, and stationery captured from the Arabs. He told me I was, from that time, responsible for the office and was then promoted to the rank of staff corporal in charge of record keeping and supervision of food stores and rationing. I was very glad to take up a job that involved writing again. I sprang into attention and saluted. Commander Simon Jada returned the salute and asked me to stand at ease and start work. In stature, Major Simon Jada was a small-bodied man with deceptively small hands but strong arms which could make men think he was a boxer. Indeed, he was a boxer in Uganda, but left it when he was knocked off and then fled straight into South Sudan to join the Anyanya. From colonial times, many southerners went to Uganda to work in the sugar cane farms owned by the Indians. However, many returned to South Sudan to join the movement.

The 1965 Juba and Wau Massacres

When Prime Minister Mohammed Ahmed Mahgoub came to power in the elections of 1965/6, a coalition government was formed. This period ushered in an increased repression in the South by the Arabs. Orders from the office of the Prime Minister were sent to all military commanders to arrest, shoot, or kill South Sudanese politicians or rebel soldiers. Troop reinforcements were rushed to the South as fighting broke out all over the region, Juba and Wau inclusive, and many politicians were either killed or forced to flee to neighboring countries or to Northern Sudan, specifically Khartoum. In 1967/8, a parliamentary vote of no confidence removed the Prime Minister Mohammed Ahmed Mahgoub from power and was replaced by Al Sadiq El Siddiq Abdel Rahman El Mahdi from the same Umma Party of the Ansar.

Politicians Ernesto Jubara (Fertit), Eliaba James Surur (Pojulu) and many others fled through Subi Camp and entered East Africa. The case of Eliaba Surur was somehow funny and peculiar. Mr. Surur was a diminutive, small-bodied man who could be mistaken for a boy. He was a very sharp man with twinkling eyes, which signified he was a man of great intelligence. An Arab officer, sent to arrest him, approached him. He asked him about where Eliaba could be found. Eliaba replied that his father was away. The officer returned to barracks and reported that he found Eliaba's son but Eliaba himself was not at home. His superiors, who knew Eliaba Surur, ordered the poor soldier to go back and arrest the person he found earlier, assuring him that he had indeed come face-to-face with the wanted person. The officer went back to Eliaba's house to find the house locked and Eliaba was nowhere to be found. In fact, he was miles away in the Southern bushes, going toward Subi Camp.

The shooting in Wau was very chilling. Many political figures,

Prime Minister Mohd Ahmed Mahgoub.

Mulana Osman Al Mirghani, the leader of the Khatmiya sect.

Prime Minister Al Sadiq El Mahdi

elders, young men, women, children, and girls were massacred while they were attending a marriage ceremony. In total, seventy-five people were massacred (see list in annex) with few mentioned below:

1. The owner of the residence where the party was held with two of his sons who were wedding that day.
2. Mr. Doka Morgan Ali was supposed to have escaped death, but due to his bravery he refused to run away. One of the military 7-ton trucks ferrying the dead bodies to dump into a well, and elsewhere, contained the supposedly dead body of Mr. Doka. Somewhere on the way to Girinti military barracks, Mr. Haj Ismail, the soldier stopped the truck, pretending that the vehicle needed maintenance. He whispered to the bodies asking whoever was alive to jump down and run away. Four people responded immediately, Bol Majok, Urbano Ukel (singer), Jima Gilo and Hassan Nima dashed into the bush and escaped to freedom. Mr. Doka was in good shape, but just flatly refused to run saying that since all his peers had been killed, it would be shameful for him to go on living. He died heroically.
3. A veterinary doctor, Dr. Justin Papiti Ajawin, was informed by a prominent Southern Sudanese surgeon (name withheld for security purposes), who was earlier tipped by a prisoner, not to attend the party, as the Arabs were going to massacre people. Dr. Papiti just retorted that "If all the Southern intellectuals were afraid of death, how could the international community be informed of the Southern demise." The heroic doctor went to the party and indeed lost his life.[5]

---

5   The long list of names of the martyrs murdered in Wau is found in

The 112 Seminarians from Kit

As for the 112 seminarians from Kit, they entered Subi camp and were received by me and some security personnel in my office. They were interrogated one by one to ascertain that an intruder was not among them. Then they were allowed to proceed to East Africa. Among them was Dr. Funda Zebedayo Dominic, a burly intelligent personality who later became a politician. Clement Wani Konga also escaped from the seminary and went to Uganda, later to become an Anyanya soldier.

Commander Simon Jada ordered a platoon to rush to Kit and retrieve all the materials, equipment, furniture, and any other items the troops could find. This had to be done to avoid looting by the Arab soldiers. Indeed, all the items which were found were carried to the camp including the priest's cassocks and these were used by soldiers in the camp. The almighty would forgive the soldiers for that, and it was good to do so to prevent Arab soldiers acquiring them.

The Anyanya Camps in Subi, Nyambiri, Group C, and Other Locations

While Subi Camp was commanded by Simon Jada, Nyambiri and Group C camps were led by Col. Michael Loruwe and Brigadier General David Dada respectively. Lt. Col. Simon Jada reported

---

annex 6 at the end of the book.

directly to Brigadier General David Dada Logunu (Bari) stationed in Gbula on the Congo-Uganda-Sudan border. His division was called Group C (Mourta). In the neighborhood (several miles away) was Nyambiri camp, a brigade under the command of Col. Michael Loruwe, an intelligent, soft spoken but tough officer (a Pojulu), who was previously a trader. The relationship between Simon Jada and his colleagues was excellent. His superiors, David Dada, and Gen. Ali Ayume, a Kakwa, (allegedly a brother or relative of Gen. Idi Amin, former President of Uganda), Gen. Ali Gbatala, his colleagues, and subordinates admired him and his leadership.

The following are the officers and Non-commissioned officers under the command of Loruwe:

1. Lt. Col. James Loro (Bari), commanding a camp near Lainya. He gave the Arabs a hard time at Lainya making them unable to move even a mile from their barracks.
2. Capt. Hitler Bali Jambu, (Yangwara).
3. Capt. Emmanuel Waga, (Kakwa).
4. Capt. Jackson Jejen Abel, (Yangwara).
5. Major Benjamin Abaye, (Kakwa).
6. Major Hillary Baba, (Lugbara).
7. Capt. January Kaden, (Pojulu).
8. Officer Marko Yokwe Musa, (Pojulu).
9. Officer Samuel Lasu (Lotole), (Pojulu).
10. Officer Joseph Kwaje (Kakwa), promoted later to the rank of colonel in the Sudanese army.
11. Officer Ephraim Hilal (Pojulu) promoted later to Lt. Colonel in the Sudanese Army.

12. 1st Lt. Edward Lomude (Pojulu) integrated as major in the Army and then brigadier general in the wildlife forces.
13. 1st Lt. Anjelo Butich (Mundari), promoted later to a senior military position.
14. 2nd Lt. Benjamin Pitia Matayo, promoted to colonel in the Sudanese Army.
15. Major Mathew, in Torre.
16. Capt. Milton Morocco.

Non-Commissioned Officers

1. Christopher Wani Kaya (Yangwara) was an artist who composed revolutionary songs calling for south Sudanese not to let their motherland be robbed. He was assigned to handle a big gun in the artillery unit. He participated in many ambushes on the Juba-Yei road. He is still alive.
2. Private John Loyo Nimaya (Yangwara), tough, deceptively thin, and tall, was a gun repairer and could assemble a weapon and dismantle it at any time. He was a notorious man and was imprisoned many times. He could run away from Yei barracks and appear in Juba. Eventually, he was enthroned as paramount Chief of Rokon, replacing his brother who was inefficient. He ruled the people in Rokon and Juba successfully and was respected by all, including the Arabs in the South. He used to cane or lash those who misbehaved with people's wives or daughters, the Arab soldiers, and civilians inclusive. He also managed to release many people arrested and taken to the

White House torture chambers.
3. Corporal Benjamina Mogo a walrus mustached Yangwara elderly grandfather who considered Nyambiri camp as his personal property. He gave good and fruitful advice to the camp commanders and soldiers.
4. Private Emmanuel Maju, (He became a Yangwara chief in Khartoum).
5. Private Joseph Gwaki, (Yangwara Chief at Rokon).
6. Private El Hai Stephano, previously a scout.
7. Private Anania Remo, previously a scout.
8. Private Hassan Apollo, previously a scout.
9. Private Lujang Elisa, previously a scout.
10. Private Sebit Logule Lujang Jerenga (Yangwara) was an excellent singer, composing revolutionary songs and was praised for his talents. He was mistakenly killed outside Yei by the Anyanya soldiers who thought he was a traitor. When rescuers rushed to free him, they found he was already dead. The guerrillas mourned him so much.
11. Eluzai Guya (Gbotoro), a Kakwa, who would kill at any time, must be mentioned. Soldiers were advised not to go in front of him as his desire to kill would emerge at any time and he would just shoot to kill. When assigned to accompany a released prisoner home, he would be warned seriously not to harm the person. His question would be "But if he/she runs away, what should I do"? He was indeed blood thirsty.

It is important to elaborate on the administrative side of the Anyanya movement. In the Central Command, Brigadier General David Dada was the Military Commander. Hon. James Eliaba Surur was appointed the governor of areas in the Central Command. Politician Daniel Jumi was a Senior Advisor to the leadership of the movement in the area. Junior staff were appointed to all the areas of the Central Command, and they were called Commissioners or Civil Military Administrative Officers. One such appointees was Samuel Swaka Yibi, a Yangwara/Mundari appointed in Saigon Camp covering Terekaka-Tali County.

There were also many people who joined the movement in Nyambiri.

Captain Francis Mori, a Yangwara from Dollo, was another officer in Group "C" camp in Mourta. He was adjutant to Brigadier General David Dada, the overall commander of the Central Command. He was a tough guerrilla officer who eventually lost his leg in an ambush. He passed on at a later stage when he had been integrated into the government army after the Addis Ababa Agreement.

Elsewhere in Tore and Koro'be, Commander Phillip Angutua was placed in charge of these camps.

Of very prominent importance is Gen. Peter Cirillo Swaka, a lean, but tough, intelligent, flamboyant soldier. Gen. Cirillo joined the Anyanya as lieutenant in the prisons in Yambio. He progressed in the bush and became a colonel in Group C. (Mourta). After the Addis Ababa Agreement, he was promoted to the rank of General and made Commander of Division One in the South and later the Governor of Equatoria Region. He became a Member of Parliament in independent South Sudan and sadly passed on in November 2019.

At the same time, Captain Joseph Kisanga (Police), a friend to Gen. Peter Cirillo, was murdered by the Arab soldiers in 1965 in Yambio. This prompted Cirillo and some colleagues to defect to the Anyanya.

Let me discuss a little about Eastern Equatoria. The camps in Eastern Equatoria were commanded by the following officers:

1. Gen. Emideo Tapeng Lodongi. After release from prison, he went straight to the Anyanya and claimed the leadership. He toured all the Anyanya camps in Central and Eastern Equatoria including Subi. He was later ousted by General Joseph Lagu.
2. A young, diminutive career soldier Gen. Joseph Lagu, a Madi seized power from General Tapeng Lodongi. He established his headquarters at Owingybul. He also toured the Anyanya camps all over Central and Eastern Equatoria.
3. Officer Galario Modi, a Lokoya, a tough and well-mannered soldier.
4. Brig. Gen. Evelino Angaya, a soft-spoken but tough soldier.
5. The big burly Lokoya General Saturnino Ariha was stationed in Owingbul with Commander Joseph Lagu. Because of his size, he used to handle the heavy weapons including the Bren gun just like a pistol. He was nicknamed the Giant. He captured many areas with sizeable Arab troops near the Torit area.
6. Col. Anthony Lojigit (Lotuko) was another officer in Simuni's camp but later went to join the rebels in Eastern Equatoria.

7. Another prominent officer was Lt. Colonel Ezekiel Wondu (Madi) who was responsible for the Signal corp.
8. Captain Edward Peter (promoted later to Brigadier General in the Sudanese army) was another officer in Eastern Equatoria. In Khartoum, due to his extra intelligence in military sciences, he was promoted to the post of Chief Instructor in Wadi Sayedna Military Academy by the High Command.
9. Captain Cecilio Jamus was another officer who got integrated into the Sudanese Army after the agreement.
10. Captain Celesio Otwari was a tough officer who fought later in the 1983-2005 war as a colonel in the Sudanese Army. He managed to open the Juba-Yei road which was closed by the SPLA in the early 1990s.

Chapter Three

Military Operations

THE ANYANYA TROOPS IN THE CAMPS undertook many small-scale operations against the enemy. In this section, I highlight some of the operations. Emmanuel Yokwe, the Anyanya commander in charge of a camp in Kelige on river Kwini once organized an attack on the Kwini River (Tapari on the Moru side) in Rokon County. The Arab tanks, armored personnel carriers, and trucks were coming from Mundri via Jambo junction through Rokon on the way to Juba. The attack was so dreadful and ferocious that many Anyanya soldiers and government troops lost their lives. The army collected their wounded, buried the dead and left for Juba through Rokon. The rebels on their side buried their dead and celebrated the success they attained in killing many government soldiers.

Elsewhere in Central Equatoria province, Anyanya soldiers under Colonel James Loro of Nyambiri were assigned to attack Juba and Yei towns, but they failed to hit Juba as the artillery gun in their possession could not fire, thus the mission was aborted. However, it was reported that they engaged the Arab soldiers in Yei in artillery duels.

Individual tales of bravery at the war fronts were also heard in the camps. For example, the story of Major John Monya comes to mind. He was a tall, well-built Mundari officer who served in the headquarters and was dispatched to Tore to establish a camp. There, he was tipped that the Arabs were approaching, but due to his bravery he refused to withdraw when the Arabs attacked. He fought back furiously, but because of inferior weapons, he was overrun and killed. When news of his death reached Subi Camp, the Anyanya soldiers wept so much, especially Col. Simon Jada. John Monya was remembered as a good and friendly chap.

One day at Subi Camp, the officers were complaining that Col. Simon Jada was not participating in military operations. On hearing this, Simuni decided to lead a company of several officers, sergeants, and soldiers on an ambush on the Juba–Yei road near Lainya, in what is now known as Jebel Iraq. A company in the Anyanya is composed of more than three platoons (about 126 strong men). A platoon is about 36 servicemen (about three squads). A squad is a small unit of about 12 men. You can imagine how the Colonel looked like when waiting for the approaching military cars. A Salahdin tank led the military convoy. The Anyanya allowed it to pass. A second vehicle also passed, but the third one, a Mercedes with many soldiers, was unlucky. The Colonel released the (energa) grenade which was tied to the Gim 3 rifle. The bullet struck the vehicle burning it into

pieces. In the process of shooting, the Colonel did not hold the gun tightly against his shoulder. The butt hit him on the side, and as he ran three hundred meters into the bush, he collapsed.

As the company retreated, the soldiers passed by him but two sergeants, Stephen Soro Yousa, and Fortunato Nyijak, returned and carried him to a nearby rivulet. He was thrown into the water which made him regain consciousness. "Where am I?" he asked. They told him, "The Arabs are behind us, shooting." He recovered fully and they ran to safety. They found all the other officers and men gathered. He admonished the soldiers saying, "You are all cowards." He motioned one officer to come forward and he took his star put it on Sgt. Stephen's shoulder. He did the same for Sgt. Fortunato. From that day, orders came from Brigadier David Dada that the colonel should not go for ambushes again.

If you saw the colonel in action, you would notice that he was moving up and down all the time; never lying on his belly but checking on his troops in action. He would put his leg on the bottoms of soldiers seized with fear (to the extent that they became cowardly), pointing at the targets and ordering the soldiers to shoot.

One day, the colonel approached me and said, "You leave the pen and books and go for operations. This is not time for pens. This is time to fight the Mundukurus using bullets." It was the first time for me in combat and I looked eagerly to it. The operation was an ambush on a convoy of army trucks near Bridge 40 (that is forty miles slightly after Bungu on Juba-Yei road. Because there was a famine in the area, and food was not plentiful, we were given groundnuts to eat. The ambush was at around 11 AM. We took our positions and waited patiently for the enemy to arrive. Suddenly a military tank rolled by on the main road. "Mundukuru, mundukuru," shouted the soldiers. Thus, being alerted, we waited for the next steps in the operation. The second vehicle, third, and the fourth full of soldiers, was to be destroyed. The lead bullet came from Capt. Lokosang Samuel (Bye-stop). Three bullets rang out signaling the order to shoot. We directed the bulk of our bullets toward the road.

After five minutes when I looked around, I saw Sgt. Zackayo Luga on the run. I immediately knew our troops were withdrawing. So, I followed, but suddenly fell and soldiers stepped on my back. I felt very dizzy and could not run. So, I crawled behind a big ant hill ready to shoot anybody who approached. Thanks to God the Arabs were usually afraid of advancing into the bush. A few seconds later,

I felt a breeze of fresh air blowing and I recovered my strength. I then followed the Anyanya soldiers. The Arab G-3 had a beautiful sound – "Takun, takun." The tank released volleys of bullets, which passed over the rebels' heads harmlessly. As I ran, an Anyanya Soldier, (Sgt. Gore Sakaeit) shouted my name. I laid down quickly, ready to shoot. But after ascertaining that it was a friend and not foe, I relaxed and followed our soldiers. It was then that I processed what I had just experienced in my first combat operation. Fear gripped me immediately and I started shaking. My stomach churned and I was immediately seized with diarrhea. I defecated just a few meters away from my fellow soldiers. They all laughed as I admitted that I was indeed frightened. However, in subsequent ambushes, I maintained my composure and became courageous.

It is worth mentioning that the Anyanya did not allow women to participate in combat duties unlike in the SPLA where women

participated fully and proved tougher sometimes than men. For instance, Madame Naomi Arona, a tough, highly educated, pretty, and pleasant lady was killed in heavy fighting in Kapoeta in 1993.

The war waged by the Anyanya attained international stature at one point when foreign fighters joined its ranks. I would like to mention Col. Rudolf Steiner, a German veteran, and a mercenary. He failed to bring to the rebels any weapons and thus was expelled from the camp. He was later arrested by Ugandan authorities and flown to Khartoum under arrest but later released. There was also Col. John (not his real name), an Israeli Mossad operative who was sent to the bushes of Nyambiri to train the troops. He brought along many weapons flown by Israeli planes. Col. John ended up in Owingybul under Gen. Joseph Lagu (1969-1971). He is alive until today and visited Juba twice in 2018. He is a best friend of former Governor Clement Wani Konga. His real name is David Ben Uziel (Tarzan).

I wish to write about my mission to my village Rokon for recruitment and fund raising. I went to Rokon during the lull in fighting in 1964/65. I collected enough cash and recruited many young men including my brother Major Stephen Soro (deceased) of Signal Corps, Jackson Juma Gimba, from Rumbek Secondary School (also deceased), Samuel Kenyi Kongo from Mundri Intermediate School, Lino Gwaki also from Mundri Intermediate School (deceased), and many others. Lino progressed in his education and was awarded a Doctor of Philosophy in Physics. He became a lecturer in Juba University before his death.

My group had a very serious argument with some of the village elders who decided to pass the collected money from the citizens to the officers from Nyambiri. Although I am a Yangwara, I detested the action because it amounted to injustice. This was resolved later and new collections from the citizens were given to Subi camp. I apologized to Rokon citizens afterwards for the inconvenience.

The suppliers of food and clothing for Subi Camp were citizens and officials of surrounding villages and towns like Juba. A good example was elder Samson Kalagwa, (a trader at Rokon), the son of Paramount Chief Jambo Lou of Jambo in Amadi. A quiet, respectable, revolutionary leader, Kalagwa was arrested by the Arabs in Juba and later murdered. He tried to escape over the fence at the White House (a facility where government troops tortured people) together with Commander Christopher Dobili (mentioned earlier); but he could not make it. Dobili escaped and made it to freedom.

I wish to talk about an operation in Lakiliri. Subi was destroyed by the Sudanese army after a tip from an insider. It would have been very difficult for the enemy to enter Subi without some internal assistance. Heavy fighting ensued for several days before the army could enter the camp. The Anyanya fighters had taken away all their big guns, materials, and equipment. They went temporarily to the hinterland of Central Equatoria in a place called Sure in the Yangwara land. The camp was moved to Moli, in Southern Bari. At Moli, Elder Abdel Rahman Sule joined the camp. He was the politician favored by Prime Minister El Sadiq El Mahdi in the early sixties and tipped to join him in government as an advisor. As mentioned earlier, Sule refused. Sule used to entertain the troops with a lot of funny stories. He participated fully in the guerrilla war. His son Juma Abdel Rahman (Police) was prematurely killed in an ambush in Kaya. He had just escaped from Juba to join the movement in Subi. During the attack, he continued advancing on the Arab camp while his fellow Anyanya soldiers had already withdrawn. He was captured alive, taken to Yei, and later executed.

Prime Minister Al Sadiq El Sadiq Abdel Rahman El Mahdi wanted to spare his life, but it was too late. El Sadiq still insisted by then that because Abdel Rahman Sule was a Muslim, he should be his Special Advisor for the South. Sule still refused and continued with the rebel movement.

One day a mobile force composed of troops from Nyambiri, and Subi camps was formed to lay an ambush on Lainya-Yei road at a station called Lokurubang. An officer from Subi was assigned to lead the company. As they were waiting patiently, a convoy of military trucks suddenly emerged on the road. "Mundukuru, Mundukuru" shouted several soldiers. The situation was tense. Alas, the officer commanding suddenly fled from the scene in total fear. In so doing, he exposed the rebel soldiers to unnecessary danger. Volleys of machine gun bullets and artillery rounds were fired at the dispersing rebels and at the fleeing officer. Fortunately, although in disarray, the officer and the soldiers fled into some thick bushes without suffering any casualties. The Arabs then focused their attention on a teenage soldier called Manase Duku, who was 16 years old. "Don't shoot him, catch him alive," barked the Arab officer while chasing him into the bush. Sgt. Duku fully agile and athletic beat the Arabs in the race and disappeared into thick forest.

When news of the aborted ambush reached our commander Simon Jada, there was total chaos in the camp. The commander was roaring like an angry lion that was about to kill. A whistle was blown and the whole camp was ordered to assemble for a briefing.

I was ordered to write an urgent letter using vulgar language commanding the runaway officer to report to camp within one hour (the journey would normally take half a day). However, I did not use vulgar language but firmly requested the officer to report to barracks as soon as possible. Note that there were no telephones by then. A runner was ordered on the double to deliver the letter within the shortest possible time.

When the officer arrived at the camp after a day, he was promptly arrested and was insulted verbally. Phrases like, "You are a woman, there's no difference between you and your ugly mother," were hurled at him. "Better go to the kitchen and cook for the real men," he was told. In the Anyanya, fighters perceived to be cowards were sent to the kitchen to cook for the fighters. However, after a while Simon Jada relaxed and released the arrested officer. What he was mostly unhappy about, was the reputation of his camp due to the hasty withdrawal from the war theatre by his men. A singer among the troops composed a song degrading the officer.

Commander Simon Jada had a serious demeanor about him, making him look like was permanently sad. He rarely laughed. He would only grin occasionally. Asked why he always looked unhappy, he replied that Southern children were being tortured and that there would be no future for the kids if the Arabs were not expelled from the South.

A camp was also opened in a place called Lokiliri, where I was posted once. The fighters in the camp undertook an operation, which was an ambush laid on Juba–Torit road at Liria. A landmine planted by the Anyanya destroyed a government army vehicle at

Ngulere. The Arab army then decided to lay an ambush for the attackers who were surely going to inspect the road. When they entered the ambush, a bullet was shot into the air and all the guerrillas melted away. (Thanks to a Nuba soldier in the army who alerted the Anyanya fighters). The Arab officer got angry with his soldiers and was determined to follow the fleeing rebels. (Note that the Nuba in the Nuba Mountains of central Sudan experienced the same degradation (if not more) as the Southerners. Some of them already had ideas of rebelling against the Khartoum government).

The rebels were sleeping near a stream and their sentry was 300-500 meters away. At midnight, the sentry, an intelligent hunter, saw a fox running at full speed. He knew something was following it. He knelt and saw Arab soldiers moving towards him. He opened fire and fell into a big hole nearby. A volley of gun shots rang over his head towards the rebel position, but all the sleeping rebels melted away. The only casualty was a Sten gun, which, if lost was punishable by death. Indeed, the soldier responsible for the gun left it behind and the Arabs took it. The loser ran home for good never to be seen again in the Anyanya ranks. In the hole, the sentry overheard the officer rebuking the soldiers for cowardice. A sergeant barked back saying, "You were with us, did you kill anyone?" This is a logical point. The army proceeded to Lokiliri village and burnt the whole village to ashes but no people, were found as they had been earlier warned by the rebels to evacuate the vicinity.

Mysterious Incidents in the Camp

During my time at Subi Camp, some mysterious incidents happened. One of the incidents occurred at midnight at the river. A colleague and I were sleeping along the bank of the river when suddenly we heard women or girls swimming in the river and laughing loudly. Presumably, the sentry on the other side of the river didn't hear it. Commander Simon Jada heard the laughter and sprayed bullets into the water where the sound came from. It was pitch dark and silence gripped the atmosphere. Again, the swimming and laughter resumed, and we both had to tolerate it until the morning. People believed that those were not human beings but ghosts. When asked, the sentry on the other side of the river said that he did not hear any sound.

The second incident happened when a young soldier was fishing in the river, where he caught a small (tilapia) fish using a hook. As he was about to pull it out, a voice came from the fish begging the soldier not to take it away as it had children to take care of. The guy dropped the fish and ran as fast as he could. He related the story and presumably, it was a mistake to do so. He died shortly after. It was believed that had he not talked about what he saw, he would still be alive.

The third incident occurred when a soldier was crossing the river. At a rather shallow spot, an invisible hand gripped his foot and pulled him towards the deep part of the river. He cried, alerting the other soldiers who tried to pull him to safety, and after a struggle one of them managed to drag him out of the water. But at night, the soldier was crying at the top of his voice, struggling against invisible beings who wanted to lynch him. The following day he was rushed to his village, but he passed on after talking to relatives about the incident.

The fourth incident occurred far from Subi camp. It was in the hot water stream (Moyo Sukun) in the Yangwara land on the Lainya-Maridi road. A young man went to a traditional dance by himself, in a location located quite a distance away. When he reached the dance area, he sprang into action dancing in full swing together with many people. Suddenly, he found himself alone. He was bewildered as there was virtually no living soul near him. It was pitch dark and he was surrounded by thick and dense forest, tall trees, and tall grass. He panicked and ran fast to where the sound of the real dance was coming from. He talked about it to people and thus passed away shortly after.

There are incidents which seem unbelievable in real life but they happened. The last incident above did not take place in my presence. I heard it from reliable sources.

People in Subi believed that nothing could stop the mysterious incidents from happening except through human sacrifice. Human beings had to be slaughtered and their blood sprayed around to stop the mysterious events. Indeed, spies, those who possessed poison (kasumak), and other criminals were eliminated around the area. The incidents ceased happening until peace downed on South Sudan in 1972.

List of Officers under Col. Simon Jada's Command

The Anyanya officers under Col. Jada were few. These were:
1. Lt. Col. Morris Tombe (Bari).
2. Capt. Songa Samuel (Kuku).
3. Capt. Lokosang Samuel (Pojulu). He was nicknamed By-step.
4. Lt. Lasu Siliwa (Kakwa).
5. Lt. Samuel Gworit (Bari).
6. Lt. Alipayo Lukudu Makana (Pojulu). He was nicknamed Nuba because he resembled men from the Nuba Mountains in Central Sudan.
7. Lt. Joseph Tombe (Bari). He was a former policeman. A tough instructor who used to insult the soldiers. He used phrases like "You look like your sister in the kitchen, your physical appearance is like your mother." Soldiers would be fuming with anger but of course they could do nothing about it.
8. First Lt. Tom Mahmoud (Baka). A tall, huge, and well built man. He was a former policeman who managed to enter Uganda at Yumbe during President Milton Obote's reign. Obote colluded with General El Nimeiri to eradicate the Anyanya. Tom died later of natural causes.
9. We had also Lt. Theopilo Lopita in the medical unit. He was a nurse before joining the Anyanya. He was a Bari but being elderly could not participate in military action.
10. There was Lt. Santino Muludiang, a medic, but rather elderly and could not participate in military operations.

11. There was political officer Timon Wani, a civilian who was to disseminate political issues to the citizens. He was murdered by a fellow officer while sleeping.
12. Another political officer was Kasmiro Wani, a Bari who preferred to work in Nyambiri and Group C.
13. Lt. Peter Lado, a gun repairer and sharpshooter who was the hunter and marksman. His assistant Sgt. Terensyo Lado, from Sindiru, was a marksman and sharpshooter. Both men used to supply the camp with fresh meat and elephant tusks which we used for purchasing weapons.
14. Lt. Alfonso Gore of Billinyang village, a ruthless soldier who could kill at any time.
15. Lt. John Kamtin – a Moru, soft spoken, relatively short but a real fighter. He was handling the Belgian automatic rifle. John also died later.
16. Lt. Tsombe –A Mundari who was sent to Mundari land to form a camp called Saigon.
17. Warrant Officer Samuel Lopore. A feared Lotuko fighter who was accused of doing many immoral things but proved to be a good fighter.
18. Warrant Officer Pompeo Subek (around 50 or 60 years old at the time) was a trucker before joining the movement. He had buses ferrying passengers to western Equatoria and Bahr el Ghazal. He was a tough man but also quite entertaining. He was restrained from going for ambushes because of his advanced age but drove soldiers to the frontline using trucks, tractors, and trailers captured from the Arab soldiers.

19. Sgt. Major Niconara Wani –A Bari elder, well mannered, but tough in training. He would insult at any mistake and that earned him the name "Dum bi talatat ya balid. You move just like your sister or mother."
20. Sgt. Major Godfredo Mori (Bari) from southern Bari; sharp tough and decisive. He was a brave leader.
21. Sgt. Clement Lobera from Karpeto southern Bari; soft spoken but firm soldier and was always in the front line. He replaced his deceased father Chief Kose Gumbiri as paramount Chief of Karpeto village.
22. Sgt Wani Andrea (Bari), popularly known as Wani Tawil, was a courageous fighter and was always in the front line. He replaced his father Late Andrea Gore as paramount Chief of Tombur in Lobonok County in southern Bari.
23. Sgt. Hayder Lasu, a teenage Pojulu fighter who often went to the front line. He was very brave indeed.
24. Sgt Enock Maluk–A tough, deceptively thin, Dinka man who would be cheered when he appeared for an ambush.
25. Sgt. Ezbon Lado–A smart, handsome Yangwara chap who used to lead several army squads on ambushes with maximum success. His character and smartness earned him the admiration and love from women.
26. Sgt. Elisa Lobonya (Pojulu)–A run-away soldier from the Arab army who joined Subi. He was a soft spoken and quiet man who handled the Fal–G3 rifle. His smiles might deceive people that he was not an angry man; but he would kill at the spur of the moment if need be.

27. Sgt. Zackayo Luga (Pojulu)–Also a soldier who joined Subi camp; a well-built toughie who spoke the Arabic language so fluently like his mother tongue and gained for himself the name "Abu Arabi."
28. Sgt. Zackayo Kinyong–A Bari, young, well behaved, and very good leader who was always in ambushes.
29. Sgt. Marcello Loboka–A barrel-chested huge Bari man who was a serious and tough fighter. Loboka gained for himself the name "Gondur" meaning a huge ant hill. Indeed, he overpowered an Arab soldier at Rejaf near the River Nile in Juba, robbed him, took his gun and fled to Subi camp. Later after a couple of months, he had a physical fight with Col. Simon Jada due to his immoral behaviour with a lady. The Sgt. was punished, by being forced to stand at attention and undergoing severe beatings and punching. These beatings had no effect on him. He was standing still and groaning with anger but never moving. The colonel just laughed and assigned him at once to carry the heaviest gun in the camp the "Vickers."
30. There was also Sgt. Khereir Fadil, a Baka tribesman, a fighter who used to smoke marijuana, (commonly known as bangi), like an ordinary cigarette. He used to sip the juice from the bangi tree. He was a marksman and sharpshooter. I admired him and wanted to emulate him. He said if I wanted to be a marksman, I should smoke bangi. As I was about to put a joint onto my lips, I saw Khereir running after a fly claiming it was an elephant. I dropped the joint immediately and up to today never smoked bangi.

31. Sgt. Luko, a Mundari who was sent to recruit people in Mundari land, who were then to join Lt. Tsombe at Saigon near Tali.
32. Sgt. Gore Sakaeit, a tall, well-built tough soldier who was always on the battlefield.
33. Sgt. Venusto Tombe, a stout, well-built soldier, ebony skinned with death sparkling in his eyes which could be visibly seen by enemy troops who were at his mercy.
34. Corporal Laku Bernadino, a small but strong, short, and stout gentleman in his early twenties. He handled all the money of the camp. He would keep the cash and gold hidden in a place known only to him and the commander.
35. It is worth mentioning that a private soldier called Lomeling, of mixed race (his mother was Pojulu, and father an Armenian) was also in the camp. He was so light skinned that when he appeared in any village, the villagers would run away shouting, "The Mundukurus, the minga have arrived." Poor Lomeling would shout after them using the Pojulu dialect but the fleeing villagers would not heed to his pleas. The villagers knew that some Arabs could also speak the Pojulu language. As such he was often kept behind the lines until the villagers got used to him. One time he was arrested in Juba by the army after it was tipped by an informer. The soldiers treated him gently thinking he was one of their own. They persuaded him to show them the rebel locations. Lomeling, then in his early twenties or teens, convinced the army that he was arrested by the rebels and was badly treated and just brought near Juba blindfolded. Thus, he said was unable to determine the rebel locations. He was freed

and he worked as a messenger in the government. He spoke fluent Arabic and Bari.

There were many tough NCOs, but I would like to conclude this chapter by saying something about myself. I was only a staff corporal, but I was intelligent and probably one of the best educated in the camp (of course to the standard in the camp). I had not even completed fourth year intermediate school by then. As a young man, I was courageous but at the same time afraid that the war could last for a long time, depriving me of further education.

Other Activities

When I visited my village, I met Mr. John Tipo, a Shilluk (who later became a Medical Doctor), who wanted the rebels in Subi to help accompany his team to buy weapons from Congo. This was done and weapons filtered to Upper Nile. There was also Officer Aquilla Manyuon from Bor who stayed in the camps in Equatoria and went to Bor to train the Anyanya troops there. Officer Gabriel Gany also stayed in Subi for a long-time, gaining experience on how to establish a camp. He later left for Bor to continue with the struggle there.

A sad incident which almost derailed the unity of the southerners took place at Group (C). Col. Michael Loruwe, commander of Nyambiri Camp, was invited for a meeting of the combined force of all the Anyanya called the "Mobile Force." Sadly, he was murdered by one of Col. Emmanuel Obur's officers. Colonel

Emmanuel himself was later killed by one of his relatives called Alfred Agwet who fled to the Chad/Sudan border but was captured. Also, in western Upper Nile one of the heroes Col. Abel Chol was murdered in the Nasser area presumably by an Anyanya officer. Those were terrible incidents which would have spoiled our cause.

There was 1st Lt. Clement Wani Konga who was a Seminarian-turned rebel. He became a general in the Sudanese Army and Governor of Central Equatoria State. In the SPLA/M he was known as "Black fox," a double agent in the Army. He was a brave man and dealt a blow to the Arabs. During the SPLM/A (21) years' civil war, General Clement managed to release many southerners from the guillotines of the Arab dreaded security apparatus. General Clement would go to the military barracks with his stick and courageously order the release of victims. He was indeed shot and injured on the leg by the SPLA in a bitter fight on Terekaka road fighting for the government.

In my village of Rokon, Sgt. Venusto Tombe was sent to join me and quarter master Sgt. Major Samuel Lopore was also sent to proceed to Mundari land. In northern Terekaka, Samuel Lopore messed himself up with Mundari women. The Mundari people are quiet, soft-spoken individuals who would not harm anybody for no reason. But once provoked, they can react out of proportion and the victims would always face death. Lopore was very lucky to escape from Mundari land. He might have been tipped by a good Samaritan to run away. He fled very fast to Subi camp and when the Mundari young men discovered his escape, they tried to find out who was behind it. They could not trace the informer.

One time, they caught an Anyanya soldier who misbehaved, and they simply tied him onto a locally made bed and carried him to Terekaka military barracks and handed him to the army.

As mentioned earlier, an order was issued to eliminate all those women and men who used poison to kill people. Sgt. Venusto ordered all the victims to be gathered in a building and he started killing them one by one. I had to save some who were falsely accused. Interestingly Venusto married one of the daughters of one of his victims. Venusto was murdered later in Luri area.

There was a peculiar incident which one of the officers did in Subi. An Arab was arrested in Juba by a teenage Anyanya soldier and taken to Subi. He was tortured using hot clothes iron. This was attached on his back. The Arab retorted in Bari language saying "tikinini" meaning put here, pointing to spots on his back. What the officer did was incredible. He attacked the burnt parts on the Arab's back with the intention to chew and eat the burnt meat. Asked why he did that, the officer simply said he had suffered the same fate in the hands of Arabs in Juba. Commander Simuni grinned broadly, and the lieutenant had to be restrained from continuing with the attack.

Chapter Four

The Behavior and Character of Simon Jada

COL. SIMON J. MULUDIANG, who lived up to 1992 (date of birth not known), was one of the revolutionary leaders of the Republic of South Sudan.[6] A Bari from Biliyang, he was tough, intelligent, but educated to a limited level, probably up to village school level. He could read to some extent, but had to be taught to sign important documents, which he successfully did. He was married to a pretty, soft spoken, intelligent lady named Erika. The lady was one of the captives accused of certain crimes against the movement but were pardoned. Before Mama Erika, Simon was married to a lady from

---

6 Here, I am referring to him with the rank assigned to him in the Anyanya.

his village. He was also married to Mama Cecilia Elia Kundu, a very pleasant soft spoken pretty lady; the daughter of Chief Elia Kundu of Lainya, the sister of Hon. Thomas Elia Kundu of the Assembly (known as Thomas Clean). All his wives had children. Although late Jada was a tough soldier who was ready to kill at any time, he was very kind to his wives and children; even to other soldiers and civilians who behaved well. I was among his favorite people. Why? Because one time at Tombili, I was trying to woe a lady at a traditional dance in which I dropped and lost one bullet. This was an act that elicits severe punishment, but he pardoned me and warned me not to lose any bullet in the future. This was after one officer, who was illiterate, accused me to the commander. One of Simon Jada's guards was Warrant Officer Richard Kibo Surur, who is still alive at the time of writing this book.

During parades, Simon Jada would inspect the troops. Those unlucky ones who were clumsy got beatings. Chaps with protruding stomachs and buttocks would be unsafe. He would bark like an angry dog when infuriated and facing a traitor.

Once a traitor was reported among the soldiers, he would be identified and brought forward. The commander would bark like an angry dog, and fully infuriated, would hurl insults at the victim. "Fatin-ger-on-like. A Mundukuru[7] is among us. I will teach him a lesson." He would then jump on the victim, kicking wildly and striking him with terrible blows. (The victim was usually tied; the hands and legs together and looking like a football when swung

---

7   Local name for a Northern Sudanese Arab.

around). Suddenly, the colonel would cease the fight, sooth the victim and release him. He would request the victim to take oath that he would never again continue as a spy. He would then be pardoned and eventually recruited into the Anyanya. Sometimes the accused would prove very useful at the end. However, most of the dangerous spies were executed on the spot.

Col. Simon Jada found his demise in the hands of the brutal Arab army who killed our beloved leader together with other heroes in the infamous 1992 Juba massacre during the Liberation War waged by the SPLA. Indeed, Simon Jada was integrated into the Sudanese Wildlife forces as a corporal after the Addis Ababa Agreement (1972). Discovering his skills and experience, the Wildlife forces transferred him to Yambio to stop the encroachment of the Ambororo herders from western Sudan. The commander managed to halt the invaders killing as many as possible and saving many wildlife animals including the elephants (wanted for their tusks).

Recalling the old days when the colonel killed as many Arab soldiers as he could find, the government in Khartoum decided to eliminate him. He was arrested in his house in Gumba, south of Juba and his final words were, "God l am dying without killing more Mundukurus, please relieve our South Sudan from the Jallaba."[8] It is worth noting that he possessed an arsenal of weapons in his house, but he was taken by surprise. He died at the rank of major in the Wildlife forces in the Republic of Sudan in 1992.

---

8   Derogatory name for Arab.

Southern Officers who Perished in the Juba Massacre of 1992

List of the Victims Of 1992:
1. Col. (Police) Daniel Kenyi – Bari.
2. Col. (Police) Phillip Modi Venerato – Bari.
3. Col. (Wild Life) James Duling - Yangwara.
4. Major (Army) Joseph Lado– Bari.
5. Major (Police) Harris Lado– Bari.
6. Major (Army) Andrew Chol – Dinka.
7. Major (Prisons) Pitya Kenyi Merisa – Bari.
8. Major (Police) Andrew Igga Nathaniel – Bari.
9. Major (Army) Yohanna Jok Yiel – (Nuer).
10. Major (Army) Majur Thon Arok – Dinka Bor.
11. Major (Army) Anyuat Nhial – Dinka Bor.
12. Captain (Prisons) Francis Lemi – Pojulu.
13. Captain Simon Sasanya – Kuku.
14. Captain Archanjelo Yugu – Bari.
15. Captain Joseph Taban – Ma'di.
16. Prison Officer Khamis Mohamed Salah – Yangwara.
17. Officer Isaac Lasuba – Kakwa.

This list is not exhaustive. There are at least 30 other officers whose names are not on this list.

The civilian officials were:
1. Director Eliseo Taban of Forestry Department – Pojulu

2. Airport officer Evelino Modi – Bari.
3. Airport officer Taban Elisa – Kuku.
4. Customs officer Kennedy Khamis Ladu Jambiri – Yangwara.
5. Joseph Sebit (Darfur) – Pojulu, a senior rate collector in the Airport
6. Eng. Anthony llario-Bari in the Town council.

In total, more than 300 people, from the armed forces and civilians, perished in the massacre.

There were more than five Southerners suspected to be informants who betrayed the people who perished in the massacre. Some were allegedly later killed by Colonel Ibrahim Shams El Din, who was stationed in Juba to oversee the massacre.

Another martyr was Brigadier General (Army) Kamilo Odongi – Lotuko, who led the "Yurmook" convoy to relieve the besieged town of Torit in 1988. The convoy was forced to retreat from Liria in disarray. Odongi was later arrested and killed in Khartoum by the Bashir regime.

This powerful but ruthless fundamentalist government seized power in a military coup in 1989. By the late 1980s, the civilian administration of Prime Minister El Sadiq Abdel Rahman El Mahdi lost credibility and caused chaos in the Sudan. A senior Muslim fundamentalist officer, Omer Ahmed Hassan El Bashir, who narrowly escaped death in an SPLA ambush at Rabkuna in Unity State in 1989, took advantage of the situation and announced a military takeover when he arrived in Khartoum. He imposed Sharia Law and embarked on a systematic elimination of his opponents.

Gen. Omer Hassan Ahmed El Bashir

In one incident, he killed twenty-eight high-ranking officers and then imposed a state of emergency and curfew.

In Southern Sudan, the military situation deteriorated. Modern military planes and guns were used against the people. Many people perished during the rule of the National Congress Party (NCP). However, this paved way for the Southerners to intensify the fight against the Arabs. I recall a statement by the elderly politician, late Eliaba James Surur, who retorted that "the south had at last obtained its freedom," meaning southerners would never surrender but would fight to the finish. Indeed, the NCP government was

Deputy President Gen. Mohd Hamdok Daglo (Hamadti)

compelled to give the South its independence which was celebrated on 9th July 2011.

Today, several leaders of the NCP are today wanted by the International Criminal Court of Justice (ICC) in The Hague to face trial for atrocities inflicted by government troops on the citizens in Darfur in Western Sudan. The toppling of the NCP government in 2019 has created the conditions necessary to try these leaders. The army decided to abandon their Commander-in-Chief, President Omar Beshir, and seized control of the government. The Deputy, General Jaafar Ibn Nauf assumed the presidency, but under pressure from the citizens abandoned it and was replaced by General Abdel Fattah El Burhan. Both men NCP members. An agreement was reached between the army and the civilians that power should be shared between them. A coalition of the army and the civilians was put in control of the Sudan headed by a civilian Prime Minister, Dr. Abdalla Hamduk, and General Abdel Fatah El Burhan assisted by strongman General Mohamed Hamdan Daglo (popularly known as Hemmeti) pending elections at a yet-to-be determined date. However, Burhan ousted Hamdok in October 2019, only to reinstate him the following month in November. In January 2022, following mass demonstrations in which Hamdok was denounced as being compromised by the junta headed by Burhan, he resigned. Following his resignation, Burhan formally took charge, placing Sudan once again, under military rule. At this moment, the NCP bosses are under trial for crimes ranging from murder, fraud, and general corruption. All things being equal, they may face jail time in Sudan even if they are not handed over to the ICC at the Hague.

Gen Abdel Fatah El Burhan

Prime Minister Dr. Abdalla Hamdok

Chapter Five

The Expulsion of the Missionaries and Forceful Conversion to Islam

AN IMPORTANT INCIDENT OCCURRED in 1964. President Ibrahim Aboud ordered all foreign Missionaries to leave Southern Sudan. General Aboud then embarked on the policy of Islamizing the Southern Sudanese. The campaign was imposed on most of our officials, village chiefs, and elders; and they were warned that they would lose their jobs if they refused. Even in schools, students were under serious pressure to become Muslims. Sunday, which is a day devoted for prayers by Christians, was declared a working day by the authorities. Instead, Friday was declared a resting day, in line with stipulations of the Muslim faith. Student revolt all over the South was witnessed as a result. This was only reversed when the military government of General Aboud was toppled in 1964. This is one of the major factors that contributed to rebellion and thus incentivized the quest for separation.

In Mundri Intermediate School, although I was a staunch Catholic and an altar boy, the Assistant Headmaster of the school, somebody called Abdel Gadir pressurized me to embrace Islam and indeed gave me the name El Hag. I shed tears of anger and accused him to the parish priest, Father Alex, who picked up a bitter quarrel with the Assistant Headmaster. Suffice to say, I did not become a Muslim but some students succumbed.

Islam is a heavenly religion, and it is just like any other recognized world religion. Adherents of Islam and Christianity believe in one God, and they should respect each other's religion. What is abhorrent is the use of force to compel others to embrace religion.

Such were the series of protracted events which compelled the south Sudanese populace to pick up arms and fight ultimately for survival as a people deserving recognition in this world.

The Relationship Between the Anyanya and Idi Amin

I would not like to miss mentioning the warm and later sour relations between General Amin's government and the rebel Anyanya movement. It was imperative that the rebel movement should make good relations with neighbors and that was why Uganda, the nearest neighbor to South of Sudan, was in the rebels' mind.

General Idi Amin Dada, later promoted to Field Marshal, was a very popular leader in the beginning when he ousted the Ugandan

dictator Milton Obote. He was a tall, burly general, who towered over everybody. Amin was the only African Head of State who recognized the Anyanya movement perhaps due to his relationship with Commander Ali Ayume of Group C camp, being a Kakwa, or because of Dr. Milton Obote's enmity towards the Southern Sudanese movement. Of greater significance may be his marriage to the daughter of the South Sudanese prominent politician, Mr. Phillip Yengkeji, who lived in Uganda all his life. The tall, beautiful lady called Christine Madi Phillip Yengkeji, became an outstanding politician in South Sudan. Amin visited Owingybul several times and promised assistance.

Indeed, Israeli weapons, materials and equipment were ferried discreetly through Kampala to Owingybul. Rebel commanders and soldiers passed freely into Ugandan territory to bring food and weapons. Southern students rushed to Uganda in their thousands in search of education which they achieved.

However, there was suddenly an anti-clockwise turn of events. Relations between the Southern Sudanese rebellion and Amin's government deteriorated. The deterioration in relations was attributed to millions of dollars in assistance from Arab regimes, led by the flamboyant Libyan leader, Muammar Ghaddafi, to Uganda. Arab governments watched with disdain, the close ties between Amin's government and the state of Israel. According to the Arabs in the Middle East, this relationship ought to be dismantled and it was indeed accomplished successfully.

Amin's popularity suddenly plummeted to its lowest degree and the dictator embarked on a reign of terror against his people. Many Ugandans, especially the intelligentsia became victims of that campaign. They were either killed or sent to prisons to die slowly under terribly squalid conditions.

General Amin used security officers from his dreaded State Research Bureau and the Public Safety Unit. Men like Officer James Wani Reubena (popularly known as Limbo meaning he would send a victim to limbo straightaway), Officer Juma Boutabika (Juma Woka), Colonel Maliyamungu (the wealth of God); who was hardly seen without a cigarette dangling between his lips; officer Bennet Kibos Tadayo; sent later to Egypt as Military Attaché; and officer Richard Songo (Ricardo), were some of the prominent employees in Amin's security apparatus. Infantry and tank commanders also supported General Amin. These include Moses Ali (from the Sudan/Uganda border), Brigadier General Charles Arube (later killed in an attempted coup he tried to make), Brigadier General Marile Hissein, commander of the feared Military Police, Colonel Godwin Sule (killed later in the Tanzanian invasion of Uganda), Officer Gibril Ali Juma, a tank commander, Ali Singo, Osman Hassanein, and many others mainly from West Nile, the Buganda region, and South Sudanese.

General Amin was toppled by Ugandan exiles assisted by Tanzania in 1979 after ruling for eight years (1971 to 1979).

The Addis Ababa Agreement and the Southern Sudan Regional Government (1972-1983)

As seen in the protracted guerrilla war narrated above between the people of South Sudan and the people of Northern Sudan, both antagonists realized that no party was going to defeat the other. As such the revolutionary government in Khartoum under the leadership of General Jaafar Mohammed El Nimeiri decided to end the bloodshed.

General Nimeiri seized power from the civilian government of Prime Minister Sadiq el Mahdi on 25th May 1969. He immediately established a Ministry for Southern Sudan Affairs led by one of the southern Sudanese Communist Party leaders Mr. Joseph Garang. Nimeiri's first government was dominated by members of the Communist Party. The communists vowed to crush the rebellion in South Sudan, but they were removed from power within two years by none other than Nimeiri. Their officers attempted to seize power in 1971 and install a purely communist regime, but after two

The signing of the Addis Ababa Agreement by Advocate Abel Alier (left) on the Khartoum government side and Hon. Ezbon Mondiri Gwanja (right) representing the Anyanya Movement under the auspices of Emperor Haile Selasie of Ethiopia.

days in power, they were all arrested and most of them executed, among them Mr. Joseph Garang, the Minister for southern affairs. Prominent Communist leaders executed were Shefie El Sheikh, Abdel Khalig Mahgoub, Colonel Babiker El Nur (the coup leader), Major Hashim Al Atta (the man who announced the coup), the tough and quiet Minister of Interior, Farouq Osman Hamadallah, and several other officers who participated in the coup. The overall leader of the Communist movement in the country Ibrahim El Nugud remained at large and was never arrested. He died on March 22, 2012, of illness in London at the age of 82.

General Nimeiri then appointed the advocate Abel Alier Kwai as the Minister for Southern Sudan affairs. Nimeiri was so determined to stop the war that he organized to meet the rebel commanders through the church. The General devised new policies for southern Sudan. He recognized the historical, social, and cultural diversities between the two peoples in the vast Sudanese nation. He particularly accepted the fact that the south was different from the north in all aspects of life that is culturally, socially, and religiously. His government decided to grant the south self-rule which was to be called "the southern Sudan Regional, autonomous government" with its headquarters in Juba.

At the same time, there was a question posing itself in the Anyanya circles as to whether it was fruitful to continue with the civil war in the Sudan or stop it. Furthermore, and what gains would the southerners achieve if they continued with the war? The answers are contained in the following three reasons:

1. Our people were growing tired. There was no substantial assistance from abroad. Food was scarce, no clothes, no medicines and morale among the soldiers was running very low. The number of deserters was increasing daily. Therefore, there was no reason to continue with the war.
2. The above was because there was no recognition of the movement by any nation, except a thin acceptance by Israel the Jewish State in the Middle East. The Israelis, because of their friction

with the Arabs, Sudan inclusive, maintained a degree of recognition towards the Southern Sudanese cause. This accounted for why they started ferrying weapons to the Anyanya and accepted to train many officers in Israel and Ethiopia sponsored by the Israeli government. Some of these officers were Captain Jackson Jejen Abel (infantry), Officer Christopher Dobili (infantry), Officer Clement Wani Konga (infantry), Lieutenant Stephen Soro Yousa (Signals) and others. The lack of recognition by many states forced the rebels to accept negotiations for peace with the government in Khartoum.

3. The third reason why the rebels were eventually discouraged to continue with the war was the support from General Idi Amin Dada President of Uganda (1969-1979) who was their staunch supporter. As mentioned earlier, he was a popular leader in the beginning when he ousted Milton Obote in 1971. He was the only African leader to recognize the Anyanya movement perhaps due to his relationship with Commander Ali Ayume of Group C in Mourta, who was a fellow Kakwa, or because of Obote's enmity towards the Southern Sudanese movement. The support eventually dwindled and ceased completely, and the recognition turned to enmity; thus, forcing the rebels to accept talks with the Khartoum government.

When the two sides felt that it was time to negotiate with each other, the church spearheaded the negotiations, acting as brokers between the political wing of the Anyanya, the Southern Sudan Liberation Army and the Sudanese government.

In the proceeding discussion, I wish to digress and talk about the reorganization of the Anyanya under General Joseph Lagu Yanga who seized command from the leadership of the scattered Anyanya forces in 1969/70.

There was a brigade under Brigadier General David Dada (Vitorio Logunu) comprising of:
- "C1" in Nyambiri commanded by Colonel Michael Loruwe (later murdered by a fellow officer).
- "C2" in Subi commanded by Lieutenant Colonel Simon Jada Muludyang (later murdered by Sudan's Omar Beshier in 1992).
- "C3" in Headquarters at Aloto under Colonel Ali Ayume.
- There was another brigade in Tore/Maridi area under Colonel Phillip Angutua.
- A fifth brigade was found in Western Equatoria (Yambio, Maridi and Amadi) commanded by different officers.

In his successful move, General Joseph Lagu who by then had assumed total control of the army/movement, ordered a substantial reduction in the scattered commands by streamlining promotions of senior officers as follows:
- The brigade in Western Equatoria (including the one in Amadi) was reduced and renamed the 3rd battalion to be commanded by Lt. Col. Habakuk Soro.
- The brigade in Central Equatoria (Nyambiri, Subi, Aloto and Tore) was reduced and renamed 2nd battalion and Headquarters battalion (plus an additional company) to be commanded by Lt. Col. James Loro.

- The 1st battalion was then established in Eastern Equatoria to be commanded by Lt. Col. Saturlino Ariha.
- The general headquarters of the army/movement was to remain in Owingybul under the overall command of General Joseph Lagu.

As discussed above, the Tore/Maridi brigade under Col. Phillip Angutua was merged with the 2nd battalion headquarters under Colonel David Dada. Phillip was given the rank of Major.

In a nutshell, the officers commanding these battalions were either demoted or promoted as mentioned below:

1. David Dada from brigadier to major.
2. Michael Loruwe from colonel to major.
3. Simon Jada from Lt. Col. to major.
4. Phillip Angutua from Col. to major.
5. Galario Modi was made captain.
6. Saturnino Ariha became Lt. Col.
7. James Loro was confirmed as Lt. Col.
8. Habakuk Soro retained the rank of Lt. Col.

With the reorganization of the Anyanya army completed, General Lagu had to embark on the organization of the political movement to prepare for the expected negotiations with the Khartoum government. The political movement was called the Southern Sudan Liberation Movement headed by Lagu himself. This movement was quite small and lacked the expertise in economic issues. It was good in military and political dispensations.

The Negotiations

Paradoxically, the leader of the government negotiating team was Abel Alier Kwai who was a minister in Nimeiri's cabinet. Most southerners were unhappy with this choice and indeed the African National Front leader Gordon Mourtat vehemently objected to the talks and refused to recognize the agreement made later. On the other hand, the leader of the negotiations from the Anyanya movement was veteran Ezbon Mundiri Gwonja, the politician with absolute loyalty to the southern cause.

This was the irony; how could a Southern leader negotiate against a fellow Southerner who had the same motives which was freedom for Southern Sudan. Indeed, the Southern intelligentsia felt unhappy and cheated, but the negotiations proceeded as planned. Through difficulties and many hiccups, an agreement was struck in Addis Ababa, Ethiopia, called "The Addis Ababa Agreement" in March 1972. The major contents of the agreement were concentrated on the disarmament, demobilization, and reintegration (DDR) of the Anyanya into the Sudanese Army, the establishment of a regional autonomous government led by a Southerner and a Southern cabinet and the rehabilitation of refugees and returnees from northern Sudan, neighboring countries, and the diaspora.

The DDR process started in early April 1972. All the Anyanya fighters were ordered to assemble in selected centers to start the process as follows:
- 3rd battalion to assemble in Juba and the soldiers received training in battalion 116 at Juba Customs area.

- 2nd battalion to assemble in various locations:
  - A company assembled at Kanyara near former Morobo County. It was later moved to Kimbi in Yei 10 to 12 kilometers on the Yei-Juba road.
  - A second company was gathered in Kanyungi in Loka,
  - A third was stationed in Kajokeji.
  - The fourth company was gathered in Saigon of Tali Payam where Lt. Clement Wani Konga was based.

All these companies including the Battalion Headquarters were moved to Kimbi for four months training.
- A company from 2nd battalion was transferred to Torit in Eastern Equatoria to join the 1st Battalion and were immediately integrated and trained there. This company was under the command of Major Ali Ayume and Officer Emmanuel Waga.
- After graduation, units of 2nd battalion from Yei, 1st battalion from Torit and the whole of 3rd battalion No.116 at Customs were passed out in a parade which was administered and supervised by Emperors Haile Selassie of Ethiopia and the Sudanese President Jaafar Mohamed El Nimeiri in a grand ceremony in Juba attended by thousands of people.
- After the ceremony, all units were then integrated separately into the Sudanese Army and the name Anyanya was regaled to history.
- Then deployment of the army was carried out as follows:
- One company under Major Dominic Dabi assisted by 1st Lt. Jackson Jejen Abel was transferred to Bor to join Battalion 105 under the command of Colonel James Loro.

- Another company from Torit under Captain Galario Modi was transferred to replace the company under Ali Ayume, which went to Torit.
- Then a third company from Bor under Major Yoannes Yor was sent to Yei to replace the company which left for Bor.
- The last company composed of units from all the battalions was sent to the Sudanese Capital Khartoum as Presidential guards. They were commanded by the young charismatic, tough and intelligent officer Captain Isaiah Paul assisted by 1st Lt. Kerbino Kuanyin Bol, 1st Lt. Clement Wani Konga and 1st Lt. Christopher Juma (Dobili); all tough Anyanya officers of high military skills.

The most important point is that the integration process of the Anyanya officers and rank and file succeeded because it was entirely and absolutely under the supervision of the President himself. He appointed a high-ranking committee under Brigadier (PSC) Mirghani Suleiman to expeditiously oversee the integration process until the end. General Suliman was later appointed Sudanese Ambassador to Ethiopia.

In total, 6,000 Anyanya officers and men were integrated into the country's forces. It seems unfortunate that no woman was trained or absorbed into the Anyanya/Sudanese army. From the government side, 6,000 officers and men were left in the South to join their compatriots the Anyanya to make a total of 12,000 troops as required by the agreement. The 12,000 constituted a complete division called Division (1) with headquarters at Juba.

The Commander who was on the ground, Major General Fadallah Hamad had to later hand the Division to Major General Joseph Lagu, the first south Sudanese to attain this very high position in the country's army.

It is worth mentioning that the number of Anyanya officers integrated into the Army were as follows:
- 20 officers from 3rd battalion.
- 20 officers from 2nd battalion.
- 20 officers from 1st battalion.
- Add to this figure officer Alison Manani Magaya and few others who were from Brigade HQs.

It is also worth noting that the remaining officers and men were integrated into the other organized forces (police, wildlife, prisons, and the state security). Some men were sent to join the civil service as officials and workers in various departments, depending on qualifications. For instance, the Department of Agriculture absorbed many who were not absorbed into the armed forces. Similarly, the departments of Forestry, Roads and Bridges and others absorbed many people. Students went back to complete their education in schools and in the only university in Khartoum. Others just returned to their villages and became cultivators.

Yes, indeed there was some frustration from certain elements, but generally the mood was of jubilation. Tribal dances were organized everywhere in the South where General Nimeiri visited. He was hailed as a hero and up till now there is a significant number of people who view Nimeiri as the best leader in the modern history of Sudan. This generated immediate opposition from some political circles in the North.

As mentioned earlier, one senior Anyanya politician Gordon Mourtat opposed the agreement, terming it a sellout. Indeed, he was proven correct as events after ten years (1983) indicated. The South was once more plunged into another ferocious war for independence. Gordon Mourtat's African National Front party requested that the negotiations should follow the following procedures:

1. The talks had to be held between true representatives of the people of the South, not opportunists and adventurists acting in complicity with the Arabs and their agents.
2. The talks had to take place without any preconditions like imposition of local autonomy.
3. The talks had to take place under the auspices of impartial organizations like the United Nations or the OAU.
4. Khartoum should be warned that what was taking place in Addis Ababa would not defeat the Southerners or deter them from future wars.

In 1973, a disgruntled army Sgt. Called Paul Pok started shooting randomly in Juba Airport where he was on duty. He spread bullets haphazardly sending people diving for cover. This was followed by two incidents of discontent which led to the murder of two senior army officers. One was Colonel Emmanuel Obur in Bahr el Ghazal, who was murdered by Captain Alfred Agwet, and the other was Colonel Abel Chol in Nasir in Upper Nile region. These were cold blooded murders. The army was able to apprehend Alfred Agwet, but nothing is known of the murderer of Abel Chol.

The other sad incident was the physical assault and beating of Col. Peter Cirillo in Juba Customs as he was the commander in the unit by then. Soldiers of unit 116 refused to take orders from their commander (Col. Peter Cirillo) and decided to manhandle him. Rescue forces arrived but most of the perpetuators just melted into the bush.

Finally, the High Command ordered battalion 105 in Bor to move to Khartoum on transfer. This generated an immediate violent protest which ended with a rebellion. Colonel Kerbino Kuanyin Bol, who was by then based in Bor, engineered the mutiny and Bor town was terrified. The Army HQs in Juba under Major General Siddiq el Bana dispatched a contingent of reinforcement under the command of Major Dominic Kassiano Bakhiet to Bor. The rebels fled into Ethiopia and formed what became the Sudan People's Liberation Army/Movement. Col. John Garang, who was in Bor, joined the mutineers and indeed became the leader of the movement.

All the Anyanya soldiers who were integrated into the Sudanese army and the other organized forces were given ranks according to their educational qualifications, experience, and medical fitness. Some were sent to various ministries as officials and workers, for example as forest rangers, agricultural workers and so forth. Others took up trading and businesses. It was unfortunate that Commander Simon Jada was integrated as a corporal and later sent to the wildlife department. Similarly, David Dada was initially given the rank of a sergeant in the Prisons department. These two appointments were examples of cheating and frustration. Later however, David rose to the rank of colonel in the Prisons department and Simon was promoted to the rank of major in the Wildlife department. No convincing reasons were given, because if it was due to educational qualifications, there were officers who were semi-literate, but got high ranks. Bravery should have been one of the qualifications.

It is not easy to ascertain the total number of the Anyanya forces in Southern Sudan. They were scattered all over the South and estimates put them tens of thousands of soldiers. The Arabs sarcastically considered all the Southern Sudanese as rebels including children. This accounted for why they did not separate children and women from men in their killing spree. It is true that because of their excellent relations with the civilian population, the Anyanya enjoyed great assistance in form of cash and food and public relations from the Southern Sudanese population.

The Regional Executive Council

The Southern politicians in exile and in Northern Sudan were summoned to form a regional government which was to be established in Juba with considerable autonomous powers. The lawyer, Abel Alier, was asked to form the first cabinet in Juba and become the country's Vice President, while General Joseph Lagu became the first military commander of the 12,000 troops in the Southern Division. Juba was the headquarters and seat of the regional government and the Southern Division. Abel Alier's first administration was

consisted of 11 to 16 ministers and a similar number of directors and deputy directors. Prominent politicians like Ezbon Mundiri, Joseph Oduho, Peter Gatkuoth, Hillary Paul Logali, Dr. Gama Hassan, Akot Atem, Enock Mading De Garang, were appointed to cabinet. Dr. Lawrence Wol Wol, Ezekiel Kodi, Oliver Albino Batali, Dr. Justin Yac, Nathalie Olwak, Luigi Adwok, Isaiah Kulang, Lubari Ramba and the only woman, Madame Victoria Yar formed the first government of Southern Sudan. In further cabinet reshuffles later, young and shrewd politicians like Simon Mori Didomo, Ali Tamim Fartak, Michael Tawil Ngamunde, and others replaced some colleagues. Eliaba James Surur was made the Director of Information. Bona Malual remained a Minister in Khartoum. Veteran politician Aggrey Jaden was made director of a ministry, a post he did not serve in. Politician Clement Mboro became the Speaker of the Transitional Legislative Assembly. Note that this administration was steering the South to popular elections after two years.

Due note is to be taken of the fact that tribalism was never encouraged or practiced and there was absolute respect for the government and the army. The army was friendly to people and mixed up freely with the population. Enthusiasm was very high as people expected big transformations in the country and society.

Funding for reintegration of the army was from the government in Khartoum, and non-governmental organizations. The United Nations bodies helped with the repatriation and return programs.

At this juncture, it is appropriate to list the leaders of Southern Sudan and South Sudan from the Addis Ababa Agreement to the Independence of South Sudan (1972 to 2011) as below:

President Abel Alier inspecting a laboratory in the University of Juba

- **The first regional governments of 1972 – 1978:**
  Advocate Abel Alier's transitional period 1972 – 1973. On 25th April 1972, the government took up its responsibilities which were focused on repatriation, resettlement, and rehabilitation of refugees and internally displaced. Another task was to set up the regional system of government. The third task was to prepare for the general elections which was to take place in November 1973. When elections were conducted, the results brought back **Abel Alier** for the second time. He was then declared as President of the High Executive Council. He ruled from 1974 to 1977 but had problems with the Assembly and the Army Chief General Joseph Lagu.

General Joseph Lagu Yanga took over from Abel in 1978 and was ordered to retire from the Army by the President.

- **The second regional government 1978 – 1980:**

  General Joseph Lagu was elected as the new President of the HEC in 1978. He ruled until 1980 and elections were conducted which brought Abel back to power.

  In 1979–1980, **Peter Gatkuoth** led an interim administration to prepare for elections.

- **The third regional government 1980–1981:**

  The third regional government was formed after elections which took place in May 1980. **Alier** was declared winner and he was asked for the third time to form the government. It was in this period that the wind of change started blowing and highly disappointed Equatorians and some politicians from Upper Nile and Bahr el Ghazal advocated for re-division of the South.

When President Nimeiri removed Abel Alier from power in 1981, he appointed **General Gismalla Abdalla Rasas** (a Fertit from Wau), to lead the South on an interim basis. General Rasas was the head of the Military College in Omdurman. In April 1982, President Nimeiri announced new elections for the south. These elections resulted in the success of **Engineer Joseph James Tombura,** an Azande from Tombura, an advocate of re-division. Tombura ruled from 1982 until 1983 when the re-division of Southern Sudan was declared. At the same year, the declaration of Sharia Law was announced, and the second war started in full swing.

From 1983, the three regions of Equatoria, Upper Nile and Bahr el Ghazal were ruled separately by governors appointed by Khartoum.

Peter Gatkuoth

Eng, Jaames Joseph Tombura

The first Governor of Equatoria Region was Joseph James Tombura. He appointed the diminutive career nurse Francis Wajo his deputy. Most of the time, Tombura was in Khartoum, Francis would run the region successfully. He was a tough decision maker and never minced his words. Any time the Governor left for Khartoum, Francis would make decrees dismissing or appointing people. Tombura was removed in 1985 when Nimeiri was overthrown by Suwar el Dahab.

The Fall of General Jaafar Mohamed el Nimeiri (1985)

The SPLM/A war for liberation was of course the continuation of the Anyanya movement when the Addis Ababa Agreement was abrogated by President Nimeiri in 1983. The civil war that followed was so ferocious and damaging that the leadership in the northern Sudan was compelled to call for negotiations. As this book is mainly on the Anyanya Movement, it is worth mentioning a few incidents which took place in the SPLM/A era and could be used for comparison purposes to indicate that the second civil war was much more organized and highly inclusive of all the tribes in South Sudan.

There is a negative perception that the SPLM/A war was mainly due to what is called "kokora," a Bari word signifying political division of the people of South Sudan. Yes, many people might have joined the SPLM/A because of kokora, but the real and concrete reason behind the war was the struggle for a just and good governance in a united Sudan as advocated by the SPLM/A leader Dr.

John Garang de Mabior, otherwise the south of the country would opt for independence.

In 1983, following bitter wrangling for power in southern Sudan between General Joseph Lagu and Advocate Abel Alier, President Nimeiri (probably in bad faith) decided to divide the south into three major states of Equatoria, Upper Nile and Bahr el Ghazal with governors as the rulers in every regional government. The citizens of the three provinces of Equatoria Region, led by General Joseph Lagu indeed advocated in a bitter argument for the southern Sudan to be re-divided into three regions and this was popularly called "kokora" which was hated by the citizens of the other two states. The argument for kokora was that corruption which was already deeply rooted in the machinery of the government would be greatly minimized. Every individual would go to his or her region to enhance development. It was not meant to divide the southern people as many perceived. The pro unity section of the society which was dominated by the people of Upper Nile and Bahr el Ghazal (few politicians agreed with the redivision) vehemently argued that the Arabs would take advantage of that division and abrogate the Addis Ababa agreement. If today, we analyze both arguments, I may argue that both can be acceptable due to the fact that firstly, corruption which gripped the government of Abel Alier later on, specifically in the organized forces would be minimized, if not eradicated. Secondly, development would be spread in all parts of the country and by the citizens of the regions. I can also agree that kokora would divide the people of south Sudan, a fact which indeed helped General Nimeiri to divide the south.

Carefully and tactfully, President Nimeiri, with the help of the Muslim fundamentalists and the Ansars, bravely announced the division of the south. This was of course viewed by some politicians in the south as a "divide and rule policy," and thus had to be seriously contested. This opened a way for the second war which was more advanced and had a lot of gains.

President Nimeiri had already set the wheel rolling for his downfall especially when he abrogated the Addis Ababa Agreement. To compound an already existing problem, he was deceived into imposing and announcing the unpopular September Laws in 1983. In essence, these laws were the Sharia Law of the Muslim faith. The penal code became fully Islamic. Something called the Huddud punishment was imposed and both Muslims and non-Muslims suffered under this law. Hands and limbs of offenders were amputated. Mahmoud Mohamed Taha, leader of the Republican movement, which was advocating for a liberal type of Islam was executed in Kobar prison in Khartoum. Alcohol production and consumption was forbidden; and culprits were severely punished by flogging, fined heavily, and imprisoned. Special courts and police units were instituted and assigned to deal with these cases. Most of the people who suffered were Southern Sudanese and the Nuba, the most vulnerable people who earned some income through brewing alcohol.

The President supervised and participated in dumping and pouring all alcoholic spirits from bars into the river Nile. There was no other option, except for the south Sudanese women to brew stealthily at night. Customers would approach the house with brew and quickly take their requests and get away discretely. Those customers included the law enforcement agents including judges, police officers, and lawyers, who would take their shares in tins and jerricans. Realizing this phenomenon, the law enforcement agencies devised a way of hunting for culprits. Police detectives among the Nuba and southerners were stationed in suspected homesteads. They managed to grab many unfortunate women, but as bribery was in full swing, the police would just move away. Few women were arrested and taken to custody. This indicated that the Northern Sudanese viewed this law with contempt and wanted it to be erased from the penal code.

In the port town of Port Sudan, an incident happened which could signify the gravity of the situation. A southern woman who had just finished brewing alcohol (aragi) noted that the police were on a search errand. She cooked her mind and requested her husband to make love with her when the police arrived. This trick worked very well for all the women who had alcohol in their houses. The police supervisor approached the house and kicked the door open, only to be confronted by a man enjoying himself with his wife. The police who was an Arab ran away shouting "haram, haram" to the others and ordered the cancellation of the inspection forthwith. He saw something which was equivalent to a bad omen for him and the police.

Such were the issues which made the southerners hate Nimeiri and join the SPLM/A en masse. In fact, Nimeiri's demise started in 1977 when he brought back the Ansar leader El Sadiq el Mahdi from exile. He organized a meeting with El Sadiq in Port Sudan

General Peter Cirillo Swaka

aiming at gaining support from the Mahdiya. Similarly, he appointed the zealot Islamist leader Dr. Hassan el Turabi as Chief Justice and Attorney General in 1979. Two prominent Muslim dervishes, Mukashif Kabasi and Abu Gurun managed to acquire high ranking managerial positions in the Republican Palace. Dr. Turabi had at last succeeded to penetrate the inner circle of Nimeiri's regime. Discreetly, Turabi started employing his secret security units from Islamist students and youth to parallel the government's State Security apparatus. With completion of the preparations to oust the dictator, the fundamentalists then pushed the wheel rolling.

By 1985, the Sudanese economy was deteriorating, while the war was intensifying the South. While Nimeiri was on a visit to the

United States, angry demonstrations broke out in Khartoum. The streets of the capital were full of demonstrations and riots. When General Nimeiri arrived Cairo on his way to Khartoum, he heard that his Army Commander General Abdel Rahman Suwar el Dahab had seized power in April 1985 and declared a state of emergency and curfew. He advised the Sudanese people to be calm and wait for general elections which he promised to conduct in one to two years' time. Nimeiri on his part wanted to proceed to Khartoum to confront the coup leaders, but President Hosni Mubarak of Egypt restrained him and kept him in Cairo.

Thus ended Nimeiri's reign, which started on May 25, 1969, and ended in April 1985.

Conclusion

I have tried as much as possible to offer a history of the Anyanya based on my own experience and events I witnessed in this movement. The Anyanya reorganization into an effective fighting force by Joseph Lagu will go down in history as an act that signaled to the Northern political establishment that Southerners were now a force to reckon with. Very little is said today about the Anyanya but let us be reminded that the movement opened the possibilities of achieving the current sovereignty of South Sudan. On a personal level, I am proud to have served in the Anyanya. I am equally proud of serving under formidable fighters like Simon Jada and others.

Reflecting on the achievements of the Anyanya, prior to the Addis Ababa Agreement, the number of commissioned Southern

Sudanese officers in the Sudanese Army was negligible. Although the absorbed number of Anyanya officers was nowhere near creating parity with the number of Northern officers, for the first time a visible representation of Southerners was witnessed in the Sudan armed forces. Nearly every South Sudanese officer in the Sudan in the 1980s up to the early 2000s, came from the Anyanya ranks.

The key outcome of the Addis Ababa Agreement, which was the granting of regional autonomy to the South, was a landmark event. It debunked the myth in the North that Southerners were backward in thought and incapable of managing their affairs. The democracy enjoyed in the South in the 1970s during the era of the regional government, even though the country was a one-party state, was the envy of many observers, including Northerners. Inadvertently, I would argue that the regional government bolstered our resolve to achieve our independence because it showed us that we can run our own affairs.

Today, a lot of credit is accorded to the SPLM/A for achieving South Sudan's independence. But writ large in the success of the SPLM/A was the legacy of the Anyanya in informing its actions, both militarily and politically. A careful examination of the military successes of the SPLA in the early days of the war, shows that it was a better organized force than the Anyanya. SPLA leaders were adept at messaging and attracting international support compared to the Anyanya. This did not spring from nowhere. The vanguard of the SPLA leadership was formed of former Anyanya officers. John Garang, Kerbino Kuanyin Bol, William Nyuon, and Salva Kiir, were all former Anyanya officers. Whereas the Anyanya concentrated on hit and run military activities, the SPLA avoided this mistake, noting that to squeeze concessions from the Sudan government, the force needed to capture territory. Elsewhere when it came down to negotiations to end the war, the SPLA did not want to repeat the mistakes of the Anyanya. Notably, John Garang was on record saying that he will not be absorbed again. This is a prudent pronouncement, given that the objective of the Nimeiri regime was to absorb the Anyanya, redeploy them across Sudan, and then dismantle the peace agreement. This happened in 1983 when he unilaterally abrogated the agreement. Garang observed that the SPLA should be left as a stand-alone force to protect the CPA just in case the Northern political establishment resorted to Nimeiri's strategy again.

South Sudan is now in its eleventh year as a sovereign state. Despite our internal upheavals, this is a feat to be proud of. What South Sudanese need to focus on as we move to the future, is to build their country. We need to embrace the idea of nationalism, meaning we must think of putting the country first before our individual interests. I am often reminded of my former commander-in-chief in the Anyanya, General Joseph Lagu, who relinquished his claim to the presidency in favor of Abel Alier during the aftermath of the Addis Ababa Agreement. This action required individual courage to put aside personal aspirations in favor of the collective good of the people of Southern Sudan. Similarly, South Sudanese today must always look at advancing the collective good of the country than their individual aspirations. This can be achieved by discarding nepotism and tribalism. South Sudanese must look at installing good governance and democratic principles that encourage accountability to the public and support fiscal discipline in the management of public monies. Because humans are not perfect, we will encounter challenges, including wars among ourselves. Nevertheless, if South Sudanese think of the collective good, it will open pathways to resolving our conflicts peacefully. There is a lot of potential in South Sudan, and those of us who fought for this country in the two wars of the Anyanya and the SPLA, look forward to when South Sudanese will no longer fight one another again to harness the good tidings that lie in store.

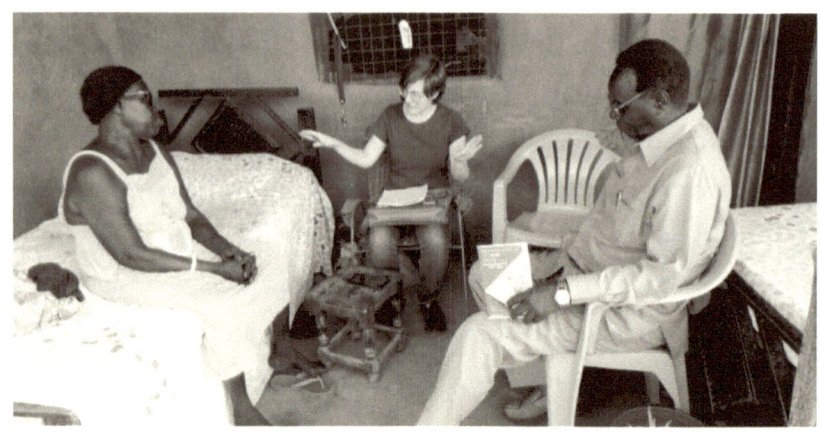

*Mama Cecilia Elia Kundu (Left), Wife of Col. Simon Jada,
Ms. Rebecca Gladdy (Centre),
American Researcher and the Author, Mr. Francis Barson, (Right)*

The bed used by Col. Simuni Jada in Subi camp

Annex 1:

Some photos of our gallant heroes who perished in Juba during the war for liberation.

Elhaj Hassan Tongo

Edward Wani Dere

Bejamin Amozia Goloko

Sarafino Pitie Luciano

Swaka Kenyi Tombe

Isaac Lasuba Benjamin

Compeo Subek

Abdurahman Sule Lukolo

Jimmy Gore

James Duling

Simon Jada

Andrew Lodu Janathan

Veteran Abdulrahman Sule his bodyguard and Col. John the Israeli

Ramadan Burai

*Note: The three left – Right are not victims of 1992

Kennedy Khamis

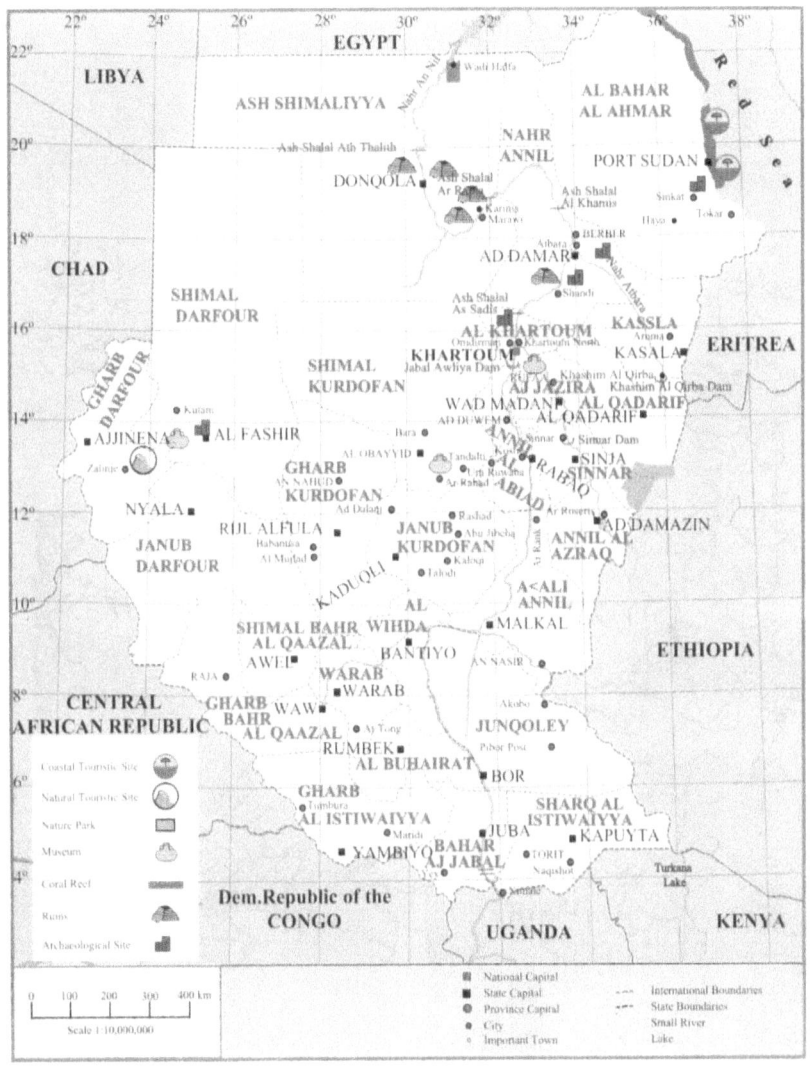

Old Sudan and its states

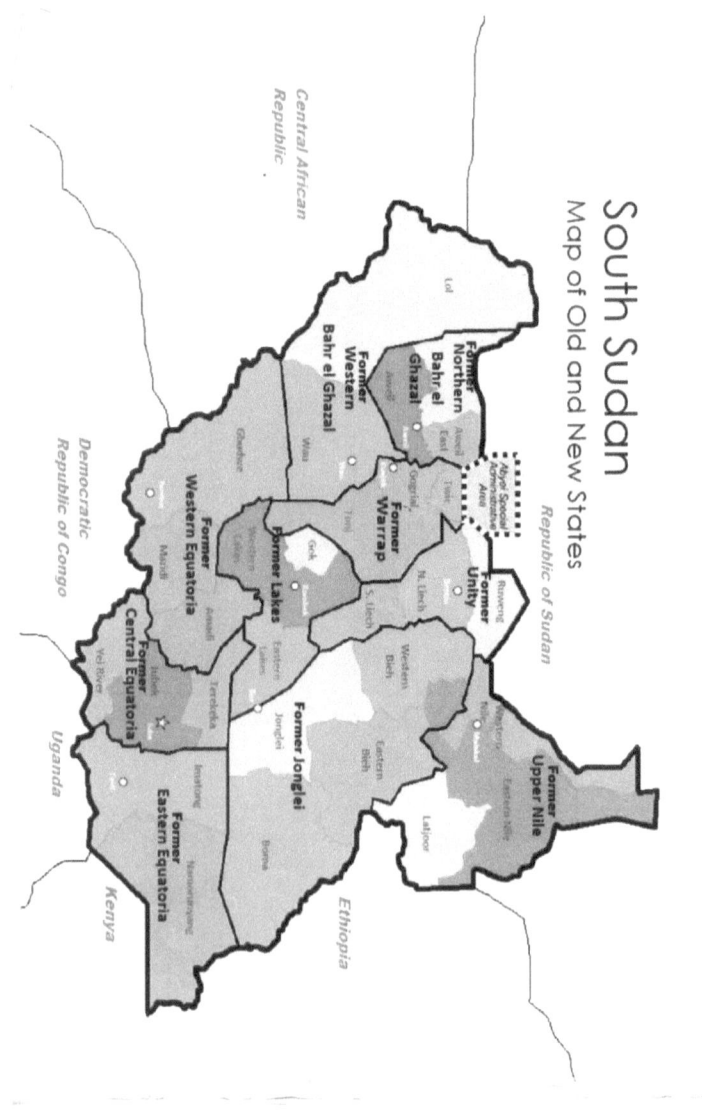

Annex 2:

Execution orders or decrees from the Arab commander of the Equatoria division to all Commanders of the security organs in Southern Sudan.

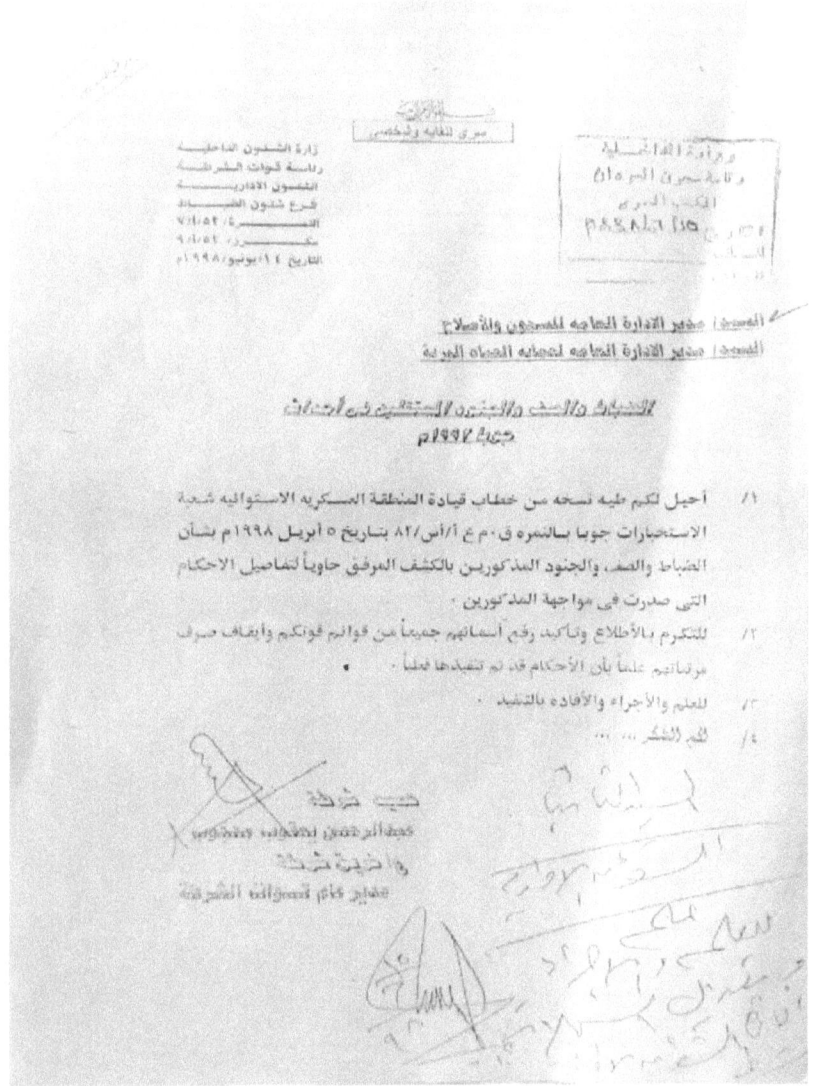

بسم الله الرحمن الرحيم

قيادة المنطقة العسكرية الاستوائية	EQUATORIAL MILITARY AREA
شعبة الاستخبارات	INTELLIGENCE DEPARTMENT
جوبا	GUBA

سري /

النمرة: ق م ح/١/٨٨ أمن/ ٢٤

Ref :
Date :

التاريخ: ٥ / ابريل / ١٩٩٨م

السيد / مدير شرطة ولاية بحر الجبــــــل

السلام عليكم و رحمة الله تعالي و بركاته

الضباط و الصف و الجنود المعتقلين في أحداث جوبا ٩٢م

المرجـــــــع :

أ / خطابكم بدون رقم بدون تاريخ و الخاص بالموضوع أعلاه .

٢ / مرفق لكم مع هذا الخطاب كشف بأسماء الضباط و الصف و الجنود الذين اعتقلــــوا
في أحداث جوبا ٩٢ و الذين تمت محاكمتهم أمام محكمة ميدان كبرى لاشتراكهـــم
في الحادث و كانت الأحكام كالآتي .

أ ــ سلسل (١) الي سلسل (٥٧)

(١) التجريد من الرتبـــة .
(٢) الطرد من الخدمة .
(٣) الاعدام رميا بالرصاص .

ب ــ سلسل (٥٨) الي سلسل (٦٥)

(١) الطرد من الخدمة .
(٢) الاعدام رميا بالرصاص .

ج ــ سلسل (٦٦) الاعدام رميا بالرصاص .

٣ / تم تأييد المحكمة بقرار رئيس مجلس قيادة ثورة الانقاذ الوطني رقم (٢٨٣) بتاريخ
٩٢/٨/٣٠م و أعلن الحكم و تم تنفيذه .

(أ مين ٢)
سري

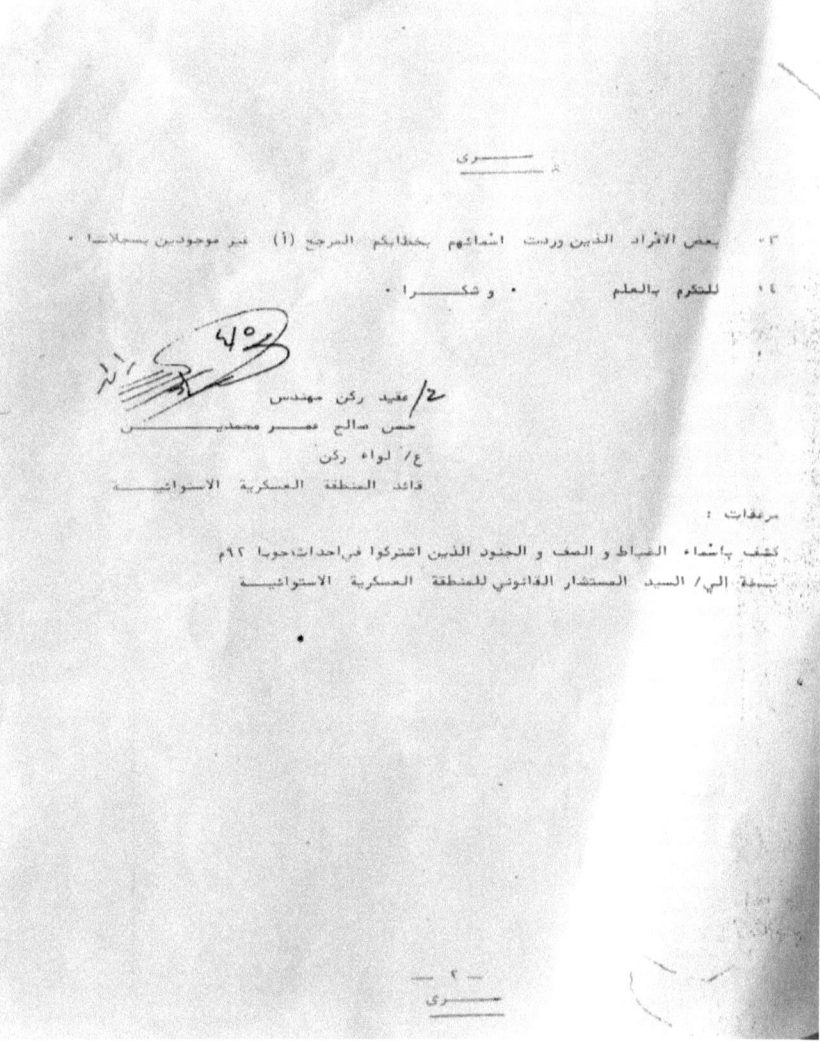

Annex 3:

Lists of executed martyrs in 1992
(in English and Arabic)

List of the Victims of the 1992 Juba Incident

S/No	Name of the victim	Occupation
1 *	Andrea Macek Kuch	Military Officer
2	Joseph Lado Lawrence	Military Officer
3 *	George John Daudi	Military Officer
4 *	Samson Gwada Loro	Military Officer
5	Martin Oluma Rudolf	Military Officer
6	Zuker Noah Said	Military Officer
7 *	Benjamin Menular	Military Officer
8	Edward Frajsla	Military Officer
9	Benjamin Malwal	Military Officer
10	Loro Sule Nyarsuk	Military
11	Kulang Benjamin Legge	Military
12	Yoanz Wani Ladu	Military
13	Ramadan Burai	Military – Accountant
14	Paul Maurice	Military
15	Augutlah Juma Kiri	Military
16	Arkanjelo Freneo	Military
17	Adriano Tangun	Military
18	Anthony Lofere	Military
19	Emmanuel Jele Lokolo	Military
20	Peter Akech Mayiek	Military
21	Mangesto Ladu Tombe	Military
22	Venansio Morbe	Military
23	Macur Thon Arok	Military
24	Kasmiro Kenyi Makario	Police Officer
25	Gabriel Bazia Fotiro	Police Officer
26	Jino Lomaru Mol	Police Officer
27	Samuel Lako Andrea	Police Officer
28	Arkanjelo Yogo Felemona	Police Officer
29	Awad Lemi Geri	Police Officer
30	Terensio Lucha	Police Officer
31 *	Philip Venazeto Modi	Police Officer
32	James Wani	Police Officer
33	Venasio Juma	Police Officer
34	Jino Awashi L.	Police Officer
35	Wilson Some Times	Police Officer
36	Amosa Lako Ladu	Police Officer
37	Hennery Ganzi	Police Officer
38	Danniel Kenyi Swaka	Police Officer
39	Marko Ladu Kasmiro	Police Officer
40	Wani Abdalla Ladu	Police Officer

41	Wani Jamos Amurai	Police Officer
42	Elizai Ladu Philip	Police Officer
43	John Salavatory Terna	Police Officer
44	Thomas Rondyang Morbe	Police Force
45	Peter Susuri Liyat	Police Force
46	James Dada Wani	Police Force
47	Satculmo Legge Laku	Police Force
48	Paulino Ladu Gidieon	Prisons Ward Officer
49	Babiker Tombe	Prisons Ward Officer
50	John Manoa	Prisons Ward Officer
51	Patrisio Wani Ladu	Prisons Ward Officer
52	Mahamed Khamis	Prisons Ward Officer
53	Mark Taban	Prisons Ward Officer
54	Joseph Taban	Prisons Ward Officer
55	Francis Lemi	Prisons Ward Officer
56	Simon Sasanya Ibrahim	Prisons Ward Officer
57	Faustino Ajsu	Prisons Ward Officer
58	Lino Wani	Prisons Ward Officer
59	Kamilo Koma Silas	Prisons Ward Officer
60	Edward Wani Dere	Prisons Ward Officer
61	Lazarous Tadeo Wani	Prisons Ward Officer
62	Anania Loful Luba	Prisons Ward Officer
63	Daniel Agoyo	Prisons Ward Officer
64	Camilo Oman Anthony	Prisons Ward Officer
65	Valantiono Lafafiyo	Prisons Ward Officer
66	Michael Akmo	Prisons Ward Officer
67	Arkadio Pitia	Prisons Ward Officer
68	Beda Maya	Prisons Ward Officer
69	Raphiel Kisanga	Prisons Ward Officer
70	Andrea Abong	Prisons Ward Officer
71	Edward Wani Duku	Prisons Ward Officer
73	Ripeni Jama	Prisons Ward Officer
74	Lino Ladu Kamilo Jada	Prisons Ward Officer
75	Pitia Kenyi Ladu	Prisons Ward Officer
76	Alberto Mamur Kuyani	Prisons Ward Officer
77	Strulino K. Kwang	Prisons Ward Officer
78	Scopas Gale Lomugun	Prisons Ward Officer
79	Valantino Ofere	Wild Life Officer
80	Pompeo Aballa	Wild Life Officer
81	William Androga David Melebi	Wild Life Officer
82	Mario Kudu	Wild Life Officer
83	Simon Jada Luti	Wild Life Officer
84	Stephen Daniel Lokudu	Wild Life Officer
85	Ben Ochi	Wild Life Officer

بسم الله الرحمن الرحيم

/ سري /

كشف بأسماء الضباط و الصف و الجنود فوات شرطة السجون و حماية الحياة البرية
الذين اشتركوا في أحداث جوبا ١٩٩٢م .

ملحوظات	الاسم	الرتبة	البطاقة	م
(هـ)	(د)	(ج)	(ب)	(١)
	أنيانيا لوقول رويـــان	عقيد سجون		١
	روينتي جاما بـــادي	رائد سجون	٣٢٧	٢
	بتيه كيتــي لادو	،، ،،	٧٠٤٠	٣
	جوزيف تعبان تيكمـــاي	نقيب سجون	٣٠٥٢	٤
	كامليـــو كومــــا	،، ،،	٣٦٣	٥
	فرانسيس ليمــــــي	،، ،،	٤٤٣	٦
	ادوارد واني دايــرى	،، ،،	٣٠٥٧	٧
	محمــد خميس صلــح	،، ،،	٣٠٧٧	٨
	لازروس جويل مدى ـــرى	،، ،،	٣٠٦٤	٩
	تعيبـان ماركــــــو	م أول	٣٠٠٦٦	١٠
	سايمـون ساسينقـــا	م أول	٣١٧١	١١
	بلنتينو لوبــايلينتو	مساعد	٧٤٠٥٧	١٢
	رفائيــل كاسقــــا	،،	٢٢٣٨	١٣
	لينو لادو كاملـــو	،،	٢٤٠٨١	١٤
	لوشيانو لبوكي ناطـــو	،،	٧٤٧٨٧	١٥
	باولينو لادو قديونـــا	،،	٢٤٢٦٩	١٦
	البرتو محمــود كيـان	،،	٢٤٠٦٠	١٧
	بازس وانــى لادو	،،	٢٤٠٣٨	١٨
	ارکاريو بتيــه لادو	،،	٤٧٥	١٩
	جون منـــوى سندان	،،	٢١٠١	٢٠
	بنحــــون اوبيجــي	،،	٢٦٢٦	٢١
	دانيال اقــوى يوتــا	،،	٢٤٠٥٥	٢٢
	جفلو جورج واني سليمون	راول واولى	٢٤٤٩٠	٢٣
	سيمان لاقــد قوتــو		٤٣٠٠	٢٤
	كامليو انطوني امــون	،،	٢٢٢٤٤	٢٥
	بابكر توميسى لوكــا	،،	٢٤١٢١	٢٦
	الامين جوزيـف منــاس	،،	٢٤٤١٦	٢٧
	بيرا مايــا كفتيـــو	رقيب	٢٤٣٠٠	٢٨
	فاوستينو اسـو لادو	رقيب	٣٢٣٦	٢٩

86	James Peter Duling	Wild Life Officer
87	Daniel Gargu William	Wild Life officer
89	Tagun Lomenari	Wild Life Officer
90	Benjamin Amuzai Goloko	Wild Life Officer
91	Ladu Sule Onarato	Wild Life officer
92	Henery Loyeto	Wild Life Officer
93	Metadio Obur	Wild Life forces
94	Francis Wani Khalifa	Wild Life Officer
95	Issac Benjamin Lasuba	Wild Life Officer
96	Nathaniel Jada Donato	Wild Life Officer
97	George William Okech	Wild Life Forces
98	Robert Wondu	Wild Life Forces
99	Taban Alisa Lodiong	Juba Air Port
100	Avellino Modi	Juba Air port
101	Kenedy Khamis	Customs Officer Airport
102	Nikson Kenyi Kupia	Technician Juba Airport
103	Sebit Joseph Lowate(Sebit Darfur)	Juba Airport
104	Moses Okayi	Juba Airport
105	Olimpio Ladu	Juba Airport
106	Tito Jamal Marona	Juba Airport
107	James Mosungu	Juba airport
108	John Joseph Kobulu	Trans Arabian airLines Juba
109	Edward Legu Duku	Juba Airport
110	Andraw Ladu Tombe	USA- Juba
111	Alfred Yoron Modi	Radio Juba
112	Michael Lobuju	Administrator Juba Area Council
113	Juma Albino	Rate Collector-Town Council
114	Anthony Hellary Wani	Civil engineer
115	Alasios Lemi Taban	Forestry
116	Sarafino Pitia Locano	-
117	Mark Laboke	Upper Talanga (Agriculture)
118	Stephen Daniel Doggale	Ministry of Agriculture
119	James Kalari Yata	Ministry of Agriculture
120	Elias Tako	Ministry of Agriculture
121	Paul Alphonse Pitia	Ministry of Agriculture
122	Salvatory Kose Jubek	Director, Ministry of Agriculture
123	John Manyanga	Director, Superi S.S.S
124	Zainab Henery Brown	Student
125	Proto Gyay	Farmer
126	James Mosungu	Juba Airport
127	Zacharia Yugusuk Tombe	Accountant
128	Modi Kamilo Wani	Petty Trader
129	Veronica Juan	Civilian
130	Philip Loro	Fire Brigade
131	Tigani Marko	Civilian
132	Nicola Jinario Lowal	Sudan Bank

133	Hassen Ladu Lubang	Air Defence
134	Jackson Lodiong Mogga	Trader
135	Philip Taban	Military
136	Yoanes Jok Yel	Military Officer
137	Micheal Mutto Elia	UNDP - Official
138	Mark Ladu	Civilian
139	John Lemi Lasu	Driver
140	Alhaj Hussien	Wild Life
141	Alfred Benjamin Laku	Ministry of Education
142	Ladu Lo Erika	Trader
143	Pitia Wani Nyambur	Trader
144	John Labic Mosa	Civilian
145	Swaka Kenyi	Ministry of Agriculture
146	Andrew Nathaniel Igga	Police officer
147	Nathaniel Jada Donato	Wild Life Officer
148	Ladu Harris Idriss	Police Officer
149	Wilson Kiri	Black smith
150	Philip Lako Vesensio Gore	Civilian
151	Sebit Wani Mathew	Civilian
152	Emmanuel Hakim Philip	Student
153	Manawa Morbe Jele	Civilian
154	Joseph ladu laki Loboju	Prisons Ward
155	Baha El dean Sule	Military
156	Wiliam Wani Joseph Legge	Teacher
157	Mustafa Abel Gadir Gari	Civil Aviation
158	Wani Barnaba Tangun	Military
159	Macur Thon Arok	Military
160	Deng Deng Wol	Military

Annex 4:

Abbreviations and Meanings of Words and Phrases

Anyanya: Madi word meaning 'snake poison' or 'wound that takes long time to heal'.

Abid: Arabic word meaning 'slave'.

Ansars: Followers of the man who claimed to be a Muslim prophet in the Sudan of the 19th century (from 1898 onwards).

Azande: One of the major Bantustan tribes in Southern Sudan west of Juba (Western Equatoria State).

Abu Arabi: Father of the Arabic Language.

Bari: One of the major tribe in Central Equatoria State.

CART: Combined Agencies Relief Team

CID: Criminal Investigation Department (Used for a traitor or Arab informer).

Capt. Captain is the rank below major but above 1st lieutenant.

Corporal or Lance Corporal: Soldier with two stripes or one stripe.

Dr. Doctor or physician or Philosophical degree holder.

Dinka: One of the major tribes in South Sudan.

Eng. Engineer.

Fatin- Ger- on- like: A clause often used by commander Simuni when infuriated.

Fal: A black heavy gun containing thirty bullets or more.

Gim: Three.

Fertit: A Bantu tribe in Wau Bahr el Gazal region of South Sudan.

Hon. (Honorable) Used for addressing a member of assembly, Cabinet Minister, Judge, Advisor to the President and to the Governor, Speakers of the Assemblies, etc.

HE. (His Excellency) Used for addressing the country's President or state Governor.

Kit: A village 15 miles south of Juba.

Kakwa: A tribe in Yei River State bordering Congo and Uganda.

Lt. Col. (Lieutenant Colonel), a rank higher than a major but below a brigadier general.

Lt. Gen. (Lieutenant General), one of the highest ranks in the army or organized forces, above a Major General but below a Field Marshal.

Lugbara: A tribe in Yei River State nearing the Uganda/Congo border.

Latuka: A tribe in Eastern Equatoria, South Sudan.

Madi: A tribe in Eastern Equatoria State.

Mundu kuru: 'Return through the river'. An Azande term meaning the Arabs should go back to northern Sudan through the river as they came.

Minga: Light skinned person with big transparent ears.

NCO: Non-Commissioned Officer.

NCP: National Congress Party, the ruling party of Omer el Bashir in Sudan.

(NYOR): Fifth columnist. Considered as rebel sympathizers or giving assistance to the SPLA.

Peng Kimang: Bari word which means quench the burning fire.

Pia Loki: In Bari meaning 'By thunder'; i.e. swearing language used by Commander Simon Jada.

Pajulu: A Bari speaking tribe found in Jubek and Yei River states.

Sgt./Sgt Major: Sergeant is with three stripes and sergeant major with four stripes.

SANU: The Sudan African National Union, a party in the 1960s.

SPLM/A: Sudan Peoples' Liberation Movement/Army currently ruling in South Sudan.

USA: United States of America.

Umma: Arabic word meaning 'nation'. It was adopted by the Mahdiya as a name for their national party.

Ustaz: 'Teacher' in Arabic.

Woro Kare: Bari language meaning 'moving on the river'. A word used for calling the Arabs.

Warrant Officer: A rank in the army or organized forces above sergeant major and below an officer.

Yangwara: 'Bull's horns' – Used as a name for a Bari speaking tribe in west of Juba.

Annex 5:

List of the south Sudanese intellectuals who were brutally murdered by the Sudanese army on Sunday 11th, July 1965 during a peaceful wedding party in Wau BG Region.

S/NO	MARTYR'S NAME	PROFESSION
1	Abderhman Achuei Apuk	*Information not available*
2	Agok Fedriok Abouk Gain	*Information not available*
3	Ahmed Dawoud	*Information not available*
4	Aldo Ring Malek Aguek	*Information not available*
5	Andrew Yai Bol	*Information not available*
6	Anjelina Ahok Deng Jur	*Information not available*
7	Athuai Maluil.	*Information not available*
8	Augustino Akile Sakeyer	*Information not available*
9	Aunt of the Bride	*Information not available*
10	Baptista Abakar	*Information not available*
11.	Bedawi Morgan	*Information not available*
12.	Benjamin Bol Tiel Yac	*Information not available*
13.	Biar Any Anch Athuai	*Information not available*
14.	Cirilo Ring Duwaar	*Information not available*
15.	Daniel Thon Ater Baar	*Information not available*
16.	Darafino Adom Rabeh	*Information not available*
17.	Dawoud Dut Chagai	*Information not available*
18.	Deng Acuil	*Information not available*
19.	Deng Rum Deng.	*Information not available*
20.	Doka Morgan	*Information not available*
21.	Francis Ring Ajak	*Information not available*
22.	Frederick Abuool D. Gai	*Information not available*

23.	Gabriel Akonon Jipr. Alor	*Information not available*
24.	Hamid Dawoud	*Information not available*
25.	Henry Ring	*Information not available*
26.	Inyasio Madut	*Information not available*
27.	James Marial Manyiel	*Information not available*
28.	John Malual Thongian	*Information not available*
29.	Joseph Dani	*Information not available*
30.	Joseph Lo K Aggwek	*Information not available*
31.	Justin Papiti Akol Ajawin	*Information not available*
32.	Kamalio Ungch. M. Hassan	*Information not available*
33.	Kon Ariath	*Information not available*
34.	Kon Dut Jook	*Information not available*
35.	Kon Kongdeer	*Information not available*
36.	Kon Mayor Deng Kl. Ariath.	*Information not available*
37.	Lawrence Malith Ring	*Information not available*
38.	Lino Ayong Monyom	*Information not available*
39.	Majok N	*Information not available*
40.	Mangar Nyuol.	*Information not available*
41.	Maria Benjamin lang Juk.	*Information not available*
42.	Mayen	*Information not available*
43.	Michael Miyar Deng Majok.	*Information not available*
44.	Michael Yai Chier	*Information not available*
45.	Mohamed Dawoud	*Information not available*
46.	Nasireldin Hassan El Reye	*Information not available*
47.	Nicknora C. Malek Deraan	*Information not available*
48.	Nyal Agoth.	*Information not available*
49.	Nyal Chan Nyal.	*Information not available*
50.	Octavio Deng M. Rehan	*Information not available*
51.	Paul Pap Majok	*Information not available*
52.	Peb Majok Yaac	*Information not available*
53.	Peter Riak Peter Riak	*Information not available*

54.	Reech Ater	*Information not available*
55.	Ring Henry Ring Jr.	*Information not available*
56.	Ring Mabouc	*Information not available*
57.	Robert Wit A. Mawein Wit	*Information not available*
58.	Salva Mawien Ariik.	*Information not available*
59.	Salvatore Biar Ayaac	*Information not available*
60.	Salvatore Kual Makuac Gai	*Information not available*
61.	Samuel Ag. Kuanyin Agoth	*Information not available*
62.	Santino Ring Ring Juuk	*Information not available*
63.	Victor Bol Bol	*Information not available*

www.ingramcontent.com/pod-product-compliance
Lightning Source LLC
Chambersburg PA
CBHW030259010526
44107CB00053B/1757